GW01090687

LESS STRESS MORE SUCCESS

English Revision
Ordinary Level

Deirdre Murphy and Tomás Seale

g **GILL** EDUCATION

Gill Education
Hume Avenue
Park West
Dublin 12
www.gilleducation.ie

Gill Education is an imprint of M. H. Gill & Co.

978 07171 84125

Design by Liz White Designs
Print origination by Carole Lynch

At the time of going to press, all web addresses were active and contained information relevant
to the topics in the book. Gill Education does not, however, accept responsibility for the content
of views contained on those websites. Content, views and addresses may change beyond the
publishers or authors' control. Students should always be supervised when reviewing websites.

For permission to reproduce photographs, the author and publisher gratefully
acknowledge the following:

© Alamy: 24L, 28, 30, 41, 60T, 62, 68, 70, 72, 74, 78, 89, 103, 106, 107, 108; Courtesy of
Cameron Anderson (cameronanderson.net): 98; Courtesy of Cartoon Saloon, Melusine
Productions, The Big Farm, Superprod and Norlum: 60B; Courtesy of The Children's Hospital
of Philadelphia: 66; Courtesy of Concern Worldwide: 64; © The Image Bank/Getty Images: 63;
© iStock: 2, 3, 4, 8, 9, 12, 13, 37, 38, 39, 40, 42, 50, 93, 94, 101, 112, 113, 115, 116, 118, 121;
Shutterstock: 24R, 25, 85, 85, 104.

The authors and publisher have made every effort to trace all copyright holders, but
if any have been inadvertently overlooked we would be pleased to make the necessary
arrangement at the first opportunity.

The paper used in this book is made from the wood pulp of managed forests.
For every tree felled, at least one tree is planted, thereby renewing natural resources.

CONTENTS

1 How is Junior Cycle English Assessed?

Introduction

The purpose of this book is to help you **prepare** for the demands of the Ordinary Level course for Junior Cycle English. It will introduce the different **assessment moments** that you will meet in Year Two and Year Three of Junior Cycle English. You will be provided with **helpful advice** to **guide you** through these **challenging** and **exciting opportunities**.

 I will learn to:

- **Understand** the different **assessment moments** in Junior Cycle English

Junior Cycle English has **four major assessment moments** which occur at different stages during Year Two and Year Three. There are two **Classroom-Based Assessments** (CBAs), an **Assessment Task** and the **final examination**. These are all based on Learning Outcomes. The diagram below gives a **basic summary** of each moment, with a more **detailed explanation** afterwards.

Assessment Moment
A moment in time when your learning is examined or checked.
Learning Outcome
A skill or knowledge you have gained as a result of your learning. A breakdown of the Learning Outcomes for the different assessment moments is found in the Appendix on page 144.

Junior Cycle English assessment moments

CBA 1/Oral Communication Task/Year Two

CBA 2/Collection of Texts/Year Three

Assessment Task/Year Three

Final Exam/June of Year Three

Assessment moment 1

CBA 1: Oral Communication

You must **prepare** and **deliver** an oral piece. An oral piece is one that is spoken.

You are free to work in groups, but you will be **assessed individually** (that is, on your own).

- You will have a **three-week period** in which to **research** and **prepare** it.
- It happens in **April** or **May** of Year Two. It is based on eight Learning Outcomes.
- Once the oral communication task is completed, you will write a **reflection note**.
- A **descriptor** will be given to **show the standard** of your work and this will appear on your Junior Cycle Profile of Achievement.

exam focus

The larger your group, the harder it is to plan the task. We recommend no more than three students in a group.

key words

Descriptor
A word or expression used to describe something.

Above Expectations

Oral Communication task descriptors

Yet to Meet Expectations

Exceptional

In Line with Expectations

We will focus more on how to prepare for CBA 1 in Chapter 2.

Assessment moment 2

CBA 2: My Collection of Texts

- From the beginning of Year Two, you will put together a **Collection of Texts**.
- The collection should include pieces from a wide range of **formats and genres**: for example, **reviews**, **letters**, **emails**, **articles**, **short stories**, etc. It is based on 11 Learning Outcomes.
- You will write a **reflection note** for each piece where you **reflect** on how you did your work.
- You will choose two pieces of work from **two different genres** to hand in for **assessment** in **December** of Year Three.
- A **descriptor** will be given to show the **standard of work** in your **collection** and will appear on your Junior Cycle Profile of Achievement.

Genre
A style or type of writing, for example horror, or writing for a particular purpose, for example a review.

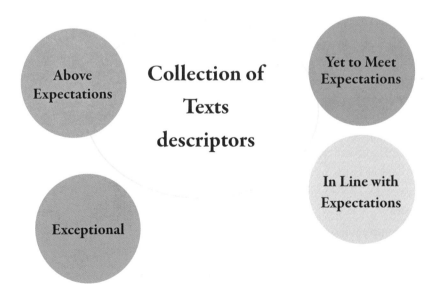

Above Expectations

Collection of Texts descriptors

Yet to Meet Expectations

Exceptional

In Line with Expectations

We will focus more on how to prepare for CBA 2 in Chapter 2.

Assessment moment 3

The Assessment Task

- This is an **in-class assessment** (two periods of 40 minutes) where you will be given a chance to reflect on the **writing process** involved in **creating** your **Collection of Texts** (CBA 2).
- It happens after you **submit** your **Collection of Texts** in December of Year Three.
- The **State Examinations Commission** (SEC) sends out a **booklet** and the **content** for the examination.
- Once completed, your booklet will be returned **to the SEC for marking**.
- It makes up **10 per cent** of your **final English grade**.

In order to perform well in this exam, you must have a Collection of Texts and you must complete reflection notes after each piece of work. Reflective writing needs to be practised like any other type of writing. We will look at this in more detail in Chapter 2.

Assessment moment 4

The final exam

- Happens at the **end of Year Three**.
- Is a **two-hour** State examination.
- The exam is provided by the **State Examinations Commission** (SEC).
- It **focuses on 23 Learning Outcomes**.
- It will be **supervised** by **examiners from outside** the school.
- It **examines** what you have **studied** in English class over the **previous three years**.

- The **questions and topics** you are asked will **vary** each year.
- It makes up the other **90 per cent** of your **final grade**.
- Your **final grade** will appear under **one** of the following **descriptors**: *Distinction, Higher Merit, Merit, Achieved, Partially Achieved, Not Graded.*

Junior Cycle	
Percentage	Grade Descriptor
≥ 90 to 100	Distinction
≥ 75 and < 90	Higher Merit
≥ 55 and < 75	Merit
≥ 40 and < 55	Achieved
≥ 20 and < 40	Partially Achieved
≥ 0 and < 20	Not Graded (NG)

Preparing for the final exam

Being nervous is **completely natural** when preparing for important exams. To **reduce stress**, you can do the following:

- **Before** the exam:
  - Ensure you **study regularly**, rather than cramming at the last minute
  - **Review** any work you do and see where you can **improve**
  - **Complete your homework** and **identify areas you struggle with**. Your **teacher** will help you with this
  - **Ignore negative comments** about the exams from others
  - **Speak to your teachers or parents** about your concerns
  - Follow the **Cheat Sheets** and **Study Tips** in this book.
- **On the day**:
  - Bring a **bottle of water** to sip during the exam
  - Pack the **correct equipment**: black pens, rulers and erasers
  - Have a **watch** so you can keep an eye on the time
  - Arrive at least **15 minutes before** the exam
  - Make sure you **read all instructions** carefully:
    - These will tell you **how many marks** each section is worth
    - They will also tell you **how much time** to spend on each question
  - Stick carefully to the **recommended times**
  - Use the **rough work areas** provided **to plan** your answers.

Below are the instructions from the 2017 Ordinary Level paper. Note the **focus on marks** available and **recommended timings**. You will be given more **guidance on timings** later in this book.

exam focus

The final exam is based on 23 Learning Outcomes. These are explained further on page 146.

The theme for this examination paper is
Following your Passions

Instructions

There are four sections in this examination paper.

Section A	Reading and Responding Imaginatively	50 marks	3 questions
Section B	Appreciating Visual Genres	60 marks	5 questions
Section C	Choosing the Words and Tone to Use	35 marks	4 questions
Section D	Writing for a Variety of Purposes	35 marks	4 questions

Answer all sixteen questions.

The questions do not all carry equal marks. The number of marks for each question is stated at the top of the question.

You should spend about 30 minutes on Section A, 35 minutes on Section B, 20 minutes on Section C and 30 minutes on Section D.

When answering on studied material, you must use texts in line with what is prescribed for 2017.

Write your answers in the spaces provided in this booklet. You may lose marks if you do not do so. You are not required to use all of the space provided.

Extra pages are provided if needed. Label any extra work clearly with the question number and part.

The rest of this revision book will help you develop as a student of English so that you can tackle the **assessment moments** described in this chapter with ease.

2 Classroom-Based Assessments, the Assessment Task and Reflective Writing

aims I will learn to:

- Examine the best way to prepare for my CBAs
- Understand the Assessment Task
- Understand what reflection is
- Learn how to give feedback

CBA 1: Oral Communication

As you have read in Chapter 1, the **Oral Communication** task will take place over a **three-week period** in April or May of **Year Two**. You must give an oral presentation for approximately **three minutes**.

Preparation and performance

In your English classes you will learn **to communicate orally** and will have lots of opportunities to **speak aloud and perform**. This is a great skill to have as it is important that you can use your voice effectively. For your Oral Communication task, you must do the following:

- **Choose your topic.** A guide for possible topics is provided in the diagram below.

An interesting sportsperson, writer, performer or film director or hobby, etc.

An organisation with which you are involved

An activity or interest or pastime you are involved in, e.g. music, sport, fashion, reading, drama, film, etc.

Choose your topic

An investigation of a text, or writer, or film

key point

There is no limit to your choice of topics. Choose something you are passionate about or have a genuine interest in and this will make the research and preparation much easier.

I've been involved in my local athletics club since I was eight, so I decided to do my Oral Communication task on that.

key point

Some students choose their format first and then their topic because they have a particular format they really want to use, for example, performance.

- **Choose your format**: the table below gives you the list of formats you can use.

key words

Format
The way something is arranged or set out.

You can use the following formats:

1. Performance	Engage in a scripted or improvised performance (drama, poetry, etc.).
2. Presentation	Create a presentation with or without notes on your chosen topic.
3. Interview	Write/create an interview situation with questions and responses. You can be the interviewer (asking the questions) or interviewee (answering the questions).
4. Response to stimulus material	Any material (visual, written, aural, etc.) could be used to inspire or guide your communication. For example, you could use a series of images to help you discuss an important issue or give your opinion on the characters in your favourite novel.

key point

Whatever format you choose, you must make sure you explore all the different things you can use to make your presentation as enjoyable and engaging as possible.

> I love drama, so I decided that no matter what I did my Oral Communication task on, it would have to involve some performance.

key words

Engaging
Something that keeps the audience's attention.

key point

You will have three weeks to research and prepare your presentation.

✓ **Cheat Sheet: Preparing for your Oral Communication assessment**

You **must**:

1. Find **sources of information** ⭘
2. **Record notes** and **develop ideas** ⭘
3. **Reflect** on your work ⭘
4. **Plan** and **script/write** the task ⭘
5. **Practise** ⭘
6. **Perform** for **approximately three minutes**, even if working within a group ⭘
7. Write a **reflection note** where you reflect on how you did your work ⭘

key words

Reflection Note
Where you note down the best parts of your work and explain why they are positive. You will also pick one or two things that you need to work on and how you will improve on them.

How will I be assessed?

Your Oral Communication will be given a descriptor. The table below shows you what each descriptor means.

Exceptional	• The communication is very fluent, and the student is in complete control of the material. • The communication has been created with imagination and has a very clear purpose. • There is excellent engagement with the audience for the entire piece.
Above Expectations	• The communication is clear and convincing. The material is very well chosen. • The communication is fully shaped, and its intended purpose is clear. • There is very good engagement with the audience.
In line with Expectations	• The communication is mostly clear and convincing. The student shows knowledge of the topic. • The communication has a purpose. • There is reasonable engagement with the audience.
Yet to meet Expectations	• The communication is unconvincing. The student does not show strong knowledge of the subject. • The purpose of the communication is often unclear. • There is poor engagement with the audience.

Top tips for your Oral Communication task

- Choose a topic you are interested in or are passionate about.
- Choose a format you are comfortable with.
- Listen to and watch examples of your chosen format.
- Make a list of things you will need for the communication and organise them early on. For example, a performance may require costume or props, an interview might require chairs, a presentation might require the use of a projector or flash cards. Keep this list safe and add to it.
- Create a map and script of how your communication will run.
- Begin practising the communication early even if you haven't completed all the planning.
- Ask your teacher for advice and guidance.

Your purpose is what you set out to do in your presentation. Are you trying to convince the audience of something? Are you giving them interesting information? Are you trying to entertain them?

CBA 2: The Collection of Texts

As you have read in Chapter 1, you begin creating your Collection of Texts in Year Two and submit your best work in December of Year Three.

Preparation and completion

- The Collection of Texts shows how you have developed or changed as a writer over Year Two and early Year Three.
- It is a great chance to develop your writer's voice and show your knowledge and ability.
- Add pieces of work to your collection as often as possible. You must choose your best work for submission at the end of term one in Year Three.
- You should redraft each piece several times based on peer and teacher feedback. This helps you produce your best work.

Redrafting – When you redo a piece of work and make improvements on it. This is a really important part of the writing process.

Reflection – Where you give something serious thought or consideration with the aim of improving it. You should complete a reflection note after each piece of written work you do. This will allow you to identify where you have done well and where you need to improve. It also helps you with the Assessment Task in Year Three.

Creating a piece of writing for your Collection of Texts – example

- You can choose, or your teacher may assign, a piece of written work, for example, a short story.
- Your teacher will talk you through the things needed to make your piece a success. This is called the success criteria.
- Write your piece.
- Get feedback from your peers and your teacher, if possible.
- Redraft your story: This is where you change any parts that you feel you need to, or include any suggestions from the feedback you have received.

Success Criteria
The things that a piece of work will be judged on once it is completed.

- Get feedback from your teacher on your second draft.
- Redraft the piece again.
- Complete a reflection note (see p. 14) and include this along with any previous drafts in your Collection of Texts.

At the end of term one in Year Three, you will be asked to submit your two best pieces of writing in two different genres for assessment. We will examine different genres of writing in more detail in Chapter 3.

How will my work be assessed?

Your Collection of Texts will be given a descriptor. The table below will show you what each descriptor means.

Exceptional	• The student's text shows creativity and complete control of the chosen genre. • The writing is highly skilled with original ideas and imaginative word choices which are perfectly suited to the purpose of the text. • The work is fully shaped for its intended audience.
Above Expectations	• The student's text shows very good control of the genre. • The writing is consistently skilled with word choices that suit the purpose of the text very well. • The work is clearly shaped for an audience.
In line with Expectations	• The student's text shows good awareness of the chosen genre. • The writing is mostly skilled, and the word choices suit the purpose of the text well. • There is good awareness of the audience.
Yet to meet Expectations	• The student's text shows little awareness of the chosen genre. • The piece lacks skill and word choices are often inappropriate for the purpose of the text. • There is little awareness of the audience.

Top tips for completing your Collection of Texts

- Keep all your written work safe.
- Get out of your comfort zone and experiment with writing in different genres.
- Save all drafts of work for your Collection of Texts.
- Ensure you complete a reflection sheet on each piece.
- Always read your peer and teacher feedback carefully.
- Don't be afraid to make changes even if that means starting again.
- READ EVERYTHING! The more widely you read, the more knowledge and skill

you will be able to bring to your own writing.

Reflective writing

So far you have heard a lot about peer and teacher feedback, reflection sheets and redrafting. These are all part of what we call the **reflective process**. This is where you review something with the intention of changing it for the better.

'There is no such thing as failure, only feedback.'

No matter what we do in life, it may go well or badly. Making a cup of tea may seem like a simple job, but even that can go wrong. The most important thing is that we look at the situation and decide how we can improve on the result. Part of this is being able to reflect effectively on your work.

Read the following short diary entry carefully and think of two ways it could be improved:

'Today was a bad day. John went to the park.'

Look at the **success criteria** for a diary entry on page 43 and see if your answers match anything from that list.

Key things to remember when reflecting on your work

Step One: Try your best!

If you don't put in your best effort, you will find it more difficult to make real progress.

> **key point**
>
> In English class, reflection is giving a piece of work serious thought with the success criteria in mind so that you can improve it.

Step Two: Ask the right questions

Before you submit a piece of work, ask yourself the following questions:

- What was the task/question?
- What success criteria were given?
- Did I understand them?
- Did I follow them carefully?
- Did I add any extras that made my work better?
- Did I review my work carefully before presenting it for assessment?

After a teacher or peer has reviewed your work, ask yourself the following questions:

- What did I do well?
- What parts of my work were highlighted for improvement?
- Do I understand why they were highlighted?
- Have I been given corrections or advice to help me improve the piece?
- Do I understand the corrections and advice?

- How will I go about making those suggested improvements?
- Are there any other parts of my work that I would change?

There is an old saying that 'Rome wasn't built in a day'. We don't become exceptional English students overnight. It takes a lot of patience, time and effort. You should always note two things you did well and try and make at least one improvement every time you produce a piece of work or carry out an exercise.

Step Three: Do a general review of your work

A helpful way to review your written work is to complete a self-assessment sheet. We have one below to help you get started on a simple reflective practice.

Examine the following self-assessment sheet completed by a Second Year student on a short story they wrote.

Self-assessment sheet

School Grange Manor Community College	**Student** *Jennifer Golden*
	Today's Date *12/10/2017*

Title of Work *The Wonderful Wall*	**Genre** *Short Story*

I worked on my own ✔

I worked in a group ☐ **with (names)** _____

Reflect on your work and then answer the questions below

(*For an individual piece of work*) **What I learned while doing this work:**

I spent a lot of time writing this story, so I know it takes plenty of patience. I learned how important it is to plan everything before I begin writing properly. I also realised that there is no harm in starting again or changing things.

(*For group work*) **What I learned from my classmates while doing this work:**

Two things I did well:

The best thing about this piece of work was the plot of my story. I followed my teacher's tips for creating a good plot and I'm very happy that my story makes sense. I am also really happy with my spelling and punctuation. I spent a lot of time checking spellings, capitals and full stops and this was very worthwhile.

One thing that could be improved on:

The weakest part of my work was my main character, Ciara. I needed to make her more interesting for the reader. I don't think she's as much fun as I wanted her to be.

What I would do differently next time (link this to the area that you would like to improve):
I would spend more time planning Ciara's character and making her more exciting. I could use better adjectives and adverbs when describing her.

Step Four: Pick specific parts of your work to improve on

You'll notice that in the final part of her reflection sheet, Jenny writes down what she would do differently the next time. Below is a page from Jenny's copy where she tries to improve the character of Ciara in her short story, 'The Wonderful Wall'.

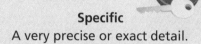

Specific
A very precise or exact detail.

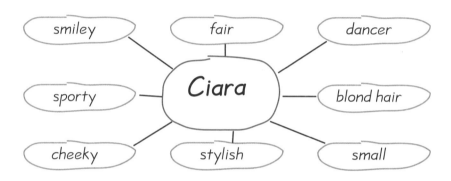

- smiley
- fair
- dancer
- sporty
- **Ciara**
- blond hair
- cheeky
- stylish
- small

Old paragraph
Ciara ~~ran~~ across the car park. She was wearing a yellow dress. Annie arrived and ~~she said,~~ 'What kept you so long?'

New paragraph 1
~~Ciara scrambled across the car park. She breathed in deeply. Her yellow dress was tossed and so was her blonde hair. Annie arrived out of breath. 'What took you so long?' she said cheekily.~~

New Words

grin

cheesy

sprinted

flicked

floral

New paragraph 2
Ciara sprinted across the car park and arrived just before Annie. She breathed in deeply and straightened her yellow floral dress. She flicked back her blonde hair that the wind had tossed. 'What kept you so long?' she said cheekily, a big cheesy grin on her face.

1. Having read her self-assessment sheet, what did Jenny decide to improve on in her story?

> **key point**
>
> Improving your writing takes a lot of work, but little changes can make a big difference.

2. Examine her copybook page. Was Jenny happy with her first rewrite?

3. Can you spot three changes that Jenny has made between the old paragraph and the second rewrite?

4. What things do you think Jenny used to help her improve this paragraph?

What helps with reflection?

- Discussing with others often helps you realise where you may need to make changes in your work. Your teacher will guide you with success criteria and corrections. Your peers can also help you see things from a different point of view.
- Reading samples of other people's work can also show you what a typical answer looks like.
- Most importantly, you must always be willing to take advice and change things if they could potentially be better.

Here are some starter sentences to help you examine a piece of work that you have written:

- The best thing about this piece of work was …
- I am most happy with …
- The hardest part of this task was …
- The most challenging thing I had to do was …
- The part I am most disappointed with is …
- If I was starting again, I would …
- I think the weakest part of my piece was …
- I could improve this piece by …
- The two things I will change are …

Read the following paragraph from Tim who is reflecting on his Oral Communication task.

Oral Communication reflection note

Reflect on your work and then answer the questions below

My Oral Communication task was called 'My Grandfather in World War II'. I started it three weeks ago. I spent a lot of time researching it and I was really happy with the way I did it. I interviewed my grandfather and recorded his answers. **The hardest part of this task was** researching more information on the things he mentioned on the internet. **If I was doing it again, I would do** any computer work earlier in the day. I was falling asleep at my computer and I didn't get it finished.

Two things I did well:

I am most happy with the presentation I put together. I had images and quotes from my grandfather on a slideshow and I used it to help me tell the story.

One thing that could be improved on:

I think the weakest part of my piece was my actual speaking in the presentation. I messed up a lot of words and sentences because I was so nervous.

What I would do differently next time (link this to the area that you would like to improve):

I could improve this piece by spending more time practising the speech part so that I am less nervous in front of the class. I could also improve it by getting someone to check my spelling and grammar on the PowerPoint.

Time to practise

Choose any piece you have completed for your Collection of Texts or as part of your class work and write a reflective paragraph on it.

The Assessment Task

Once you have submitted your Collection of Texts for assessment, you will have to complete the Assessment Task. If you have been regularly reflecting on your work through your reflection notes and other reflection tools, the Assessment Task will be much easier for you.

In order to be **fully** prepared for the Assessment Task, you should have the following:

- Your Collection of Texts with all work included.
- The **two written pieces** from your Collection of Texts that you have submitted for assessment.
- All **previous drafts** of these two pieces of work.
- The **reflection notes** you completed for your two pieces of work.
- A black pen and a pad for rough work.

There are two parts to the Assessment Task:

Part One

- You will engage with a short stimulus piece. This could be written, audio, audio-visual or multimodal. The piece will focus on writing or someone's experiences of it.
- Your teacher will guide a discussion around the piece you engaged with.
- During this discussion, you should:
  - Think carefully about the information in the stimulus piece
  - Draw conclusions about the information shared
  - Ask questions about the stimulus material
  - Consider if your experience of writing is similar to the one in the piece
  - Give your opinion on the piece
  - Listen respectfully to other people's contributions.
- The teacher will also introduce you to the Assessment Task booklet and the writing prompts you will have to respond to.
- You will have some time to consider your responses to each prompt.

Your teacher will allow 40 minutes for the stimulus piece discussion to be completed.

Part Two

You will complete the Assessment Task booklet to the best of your ability. On the following page you will see a completed sample booklet.

Your teacher will allow 40 minutes for the written assignment to be completed.

Assessment Task booklet – sample questions

Section A – Reflecting on a Text

Question 1
Give the titles of two texts, from your Collection of Texts, that you consider to be your best writing and identify the genre of each text.

First Text: `Chalkline: A Gripping Read`

Genre: Review

Second Text: `Tough Days Ahead`

Genre: Poem

Select an extract (for example, a paragraph or verse) from one text identified above. Copy the extract into the space provided below. The extract should not exceed 100 words approximately.

Extract from review:
Without doubt, Jameela is my favourite character in this book. She faces challenges from the very beginning. She is brave and really inspires me. Her father will not allow her to go to school because he does not believe girls need to be educated. She has to help her mother around the house every day. The most inspiring thing about her is that she does not give up on her brother. Family is the most important thing to her. For me, she is the hero of the book.

Question 2
Write a response to either **(a)** or **(b)**.
(a) Explain how two features of the extract you have chosen are typical of its genre.
or
(b) Identify a change that you made in the course of writing this text that you think improved it and explain how it improved the text.

After writing my first draft, my teacher gave me really helpful feedback. One major change I made was that I gave my opinions on a lot more features of the book. In my first draft I just talked about why I liked the book but in my second and third drafts I gave my opinions on the themes, characters, and key scenes. This meant that someone reading my review would get a real sense of my understanding of the book. When my partner in class read it, they became a lot more interested in reading the book themselves because I had discussed a lot of interesting things about it.

Section B – Reflecting on my Writing

Question 3

Choose two prompts from the prescribed list. Write a response to each of your chosen prompts in the spaces provided. You are encouraged to refer to specific texts from your collection.

Prompts prescribed in April 2018:

(a) How I came up with ideas for one of my texts

(b) How I worked with classmates to develop my writing skills

(c) A genre I would like to write in again and why?

(d) What a reader might enjoy about one of the texts in my collection

These prompts may change each year.

Prompt *(c) A genre I would like to write in again and why?*

Response:

I particularly enjoy writing short stories. I included three in my Collection of Texts which was more than anyone else in the class. I write them in my spare time, as well as for school assignments. There is something really enjoyable about creating characters and settings. I like to read different genres and take ideas from them. I could have a love story in the middle of a horror story or I sometimes put real people in weird locations. I once put the Pope in space. Some of my ideas are a bit mad, but that's the best part. Short stories really let you explore different ideas. I love experimenting with different vocabulary and trying to figure out interesting ways to describe people as well. I once described my teacher's classroom as a 'shapeless wreck' in a story. He loved the description, but then he realised it was about his room.

Prompt   *(b) How I worked with classmates to develop my writing skills*

Response:

We were given lots of opportunities to work with our classmates in English class. I found this really helpful because I struggle with certain parts of my writing. Sometimes I find it hard to choose the right words for a piece of writing. Working with different partners meant I learned more vocabulary. Sometimes they suggested good books to read and films to watch and that meant I got fresh ideas as well. It was also really helpful have a peer look over my work and get their feedback. It made me more confident in my ability. I always thought my short stories and poems were a bit mad, but my classmates really liked them. Sometimes we would work in groups to write pieces for class. This was an opportunity to hear new ideas and see different writing styles.

aims

aims I will learn to:

- Look for clues
- Recognise writing genres
- Be aware of different types of writing
- Read with a goal in mind
- Make a personal link or connection
- Question the text
- Reflect on the story and writing
- Use PIE (Point, Illustrate, Explain)

Different types of writing

There are many different types of text that you may be asked to read and respond to. Each text is different in its layout and the type of language it uses. Below are some examples that you may be asked to read:

Interview	→	has an interviewer and an interviewee (the person being interviewed). The language can be formal or informal, and the responses can be very personal.
Letter	→	is addressed to someone, has a date, a greeting and sign-off. The language can be informal or formal depending on the purpose of the letter.
Review	→	is when someone judges something they have experienced, for example, a film. The language can be formal or informal based on what the review is about and the people it is written for.
Drama	→	is a play and has at least one character, but usually two or more. The language is generally informal as it reflects what people say in everyday conversation. However, plays written in other centuries – for example, those written by Shakespeare – may have a more formal type of language.
Novel	→	is a fictional (made-up) story. It usually features more than one character and has a mixture of both formal and informal language.

Article	→	is an opinion piece. It can be either serious or humorous and so can have formal or informal language depending on the subject. It can have a mixture of information, statistics, quotes and opinion.
Speech	→	is an opinion piece which is spoken. It is usually spoken to an audience, has a greeting, information, statistics, quotes and opinion. It can be serious or humorous.
Blog	→	is an online opinion piece. It can be serious like an article or more informal like a diary entry.
Song lyrics	→	*are like poems. A song can have all the techniques that poems have, such as rhyme, alliteration, etc.*
Email	→	is like an online letter. It can be either formal or informal depending on the subject matter.
Report	→	is usually an investigation into something. It should outline its findings, its recommendations and solutions.

As you can see, each form of writing has its own style or genre, and some, like books, emails and blogs, can be written in more than one style or genre.

Understanding genre in books

Genre describes a specific style or category of writing in books and literature. Readers expect certain things from different genres. For example, we would expect that books in the science fiction genre will have something to do with space or could feature futuristic settings, whereas fantasy books might have magic or supernatural characters in them.

Genre types

Romance – has a love story between two people with a happy and optimistic ending.
Science fiction – has a futuristic setting or characters who have some connection with space.

Fantasy – has a setting or characters that have some connection with magic or the supernatural (ghosts and spirits).

Autobiography – is about a person's life, written by that person, and has lots of personal thoughts and emotions.

Biography – is about a person's life but is written by someone else. It usually has more information with fewer personal thoughts and emotions.

Drama – has a more serious tone to the story with lots of emotional highs and lows.

Action and adventure – has a big threat or danger and chases, which create lots of excitement.

Horror – has some connection to fear or death or the supernatural.

Mystery – has a problem or puzzle that needs to be solved.

Travel – has stories about a person's travels to different places.

Historical fiction – is a story that is based around a historical event or period.

Young adult (YA) – is a story written with teenagers and young adults in mind.

How to be an effective reader

Step 1
Before reading, you need to:
1. Look at the **title** of the text
2. Read any **background information**
3. Look at any **images** that accompany the text
4. Check if there are any **links** between these three things.

Step 2
First reading:
1. Read the **whole** piece to get the **gist (general idea)** of it
2. If there are any **words or phrases** you don't understand, try to **read the sentence again** and **guess** what the word or phrase **might mean**.

How to be an effective reader

Step 3
Second reading:
1. Go to the questions and **underline key words**
2. **Read the text again** to see if you can **spot the answers** or any of the **key words**
3. Write **your own notes** at the side of the paper if you spot anything.

Step 4
Response to your reading:
1. How did **you feel** about the text you have just read?
2. Did the writer succeed in getting **you** to **like it** or were you **disappointed**?
3. Do **you** share any **links or connections** with the speaker(s) of the text?

Successful reading in action

Read the following review of Ed Sheeran's third album, ÷, and find out what the album tells us about this really successful but down-to-earth singer.

Sample review

From the typical Sheeran ballad to rapping about Ireland's very own Galway, this album is a very mixed collection for the singer–songwriter who has previously given up social media for a year and who is Taylor Swift's bestie.

Background information

Examine the images

For such a young man, a lot of people often ask themselves 'Is there anything that Ed Sheeran can't do?' On the back of two very successful albums entitled × and +, the third album had a lot to live up to. One reason for this success is that he doesn't stick to just one genre of music. Like his previous albums, Sheeran features songs that blend a lot of different music techniques and genres such as rap, pop, folk and digital mixing. There is something for everyone on this album.

Another reason is that Sheeran writes from the heart. His lyrics tell stories about his experiences of being an average guy who has to deal with the same things other people do. He also uses family influences in tracks such as 'Galway Girl' where Sheeran gives a nod to his Irish roots. He is huge over here in Ireland and it is great that Sheeran uses that mixture of traditional music with his own blend of rap and pop to create this very catchy track.

The album also features a song about his grandmother's funeral called 'Supermarket Flowers', which is slow and pleasing to the ear. Sheeran's ability to be the superstar and the everyday man contributes to his popularity, but it would be nothing without his unique talent for creating fun songs.

That is not to say that Sheeran doesn't find his success a little stressful. He is reported to have stayed away from social media because he was anxious and overwhelmed by so many people wanting different

Key words from Question 1

things from him. However, Sheeran makes the most of his current situation and seems to acknowledge how lucky he is. He looks to popular singers such as George Michael, who died so young, and realises the impact that George had on his fans. Sheeran, himself being a big fan, was really surprised and saddened by his death.

Key words from Question 2

On the other hand, it seems that this album embraces life and has fun with it. Definitely the song to really watch out for is 'Shape of You'. This balances a great vocal performance along with an insanely catchy beat.

This album is full of pop genius, but it isn't for everyone. Part of Sheeran's appeal is the variety in his music, but I think this album might go a bit too far with that for some fans. Not everyone will like jumping from an Irish inspired hit to a simpler groove featured in other songs.

Sample questions and answers

Questions

Genre type – review

1. Ed Sheeran removed himself from social media because:
   A. He just wasn't really interested in Snapchat any more
   B. He felt under pressure to constantly help people
   C. He realised that all his time was spent on social media
   D. He was bored.

    B

2. Why was Sheeran affected by George Michael's death?
   A. It was under very tragic circumstances
   B. He was a singer just like himself
   C. He didn't want to lose another legend
   D. He was very popular.

    D

3. What does the reviewer think about the album?
   A. Hates it
   B. Likes some songs but doesn't like others
   C. Likes it but thinks that it isn't for everyone
   D. Can find no fault with the album.

    C

Answering questions

In the exam you are given lots of different texts to read and you are asked different types of questions.

exam focus

Comprehension questions can be asked like multiple choice, true or false, or find the odd one out. Below is an example of multiple-choice questions based on a movie poster.

Example
Section A – Reading Comprehension

Question 1   **10 marks**

Based on what you can see in both of the posters, write the letter corresponding to the correct answers in the box.

(a) The film *Song of the Sea* opens in cinemas on:
- **A.** The ninth of December
- **B.** The nineteenth of November
- **C.** December the nineteenth
- **D.** December the ninth

(b) As a rating, one of the reviews rewards the film:
- **A.** Four stars
- **B.** Thumbs up
- **C.** Five stars
- **D.** An Oscar

(c) The director of a *Song of the Sea* also directed a film called:
- **A.** *The Academy Award*
- **B.** *Dazzling*
- **C.** *The Secret of Kells*
- **D.** *A Beautiful Film*

(d) When one of the reviews says that the film is 'spellbinding', it means that:
- **A.** The film is about wizards and magicians
- **B.** You will leave the film feeling dizzy
- **C.** The film will hold your interest completely
- **D.** The film is confusing

Apart from comprehension questions, you can be asked anything at all – see an example on the following page. However, it is important that you remember that these questions will all be based around your own understanding of the text and your feelings towards it.

Question 2   **5 marks**

Based on what you can see in the two posters, who do you think would enjoy this film? Explain your answer.

_____

_____

_____

_____

Phrases to help you express your personal opinion:

I think that ...	In my opinion, ...	I feel ...
I believe ...	My impression of ...	I hold the view that ...
To me, ...	Personally, I'd say that ...	From my point of view, ...

Did you like or dislike something?

Words and phrases to help you:

Like

- Enjoy
- Agree
- Admire
- Terrific
- Marvellous
- Adore
- Delighted
- Pleased
- Satisfied
- Marvel at
- Respect
- Applaud
- Appreciate

> **key point**
>
> If you are asked whether you like or dislike something, it is important to try and use different words and phrases to help you explain why.

Dislike

- Hate
- Disgusted
- Disagree
- Detest
- Loathe
- Condemn
- Abhor

Success criteria for answering questions

Point, Illustrate, Explain (PIE)

When reading and responding, you must always refer to the text. Use the following formula to help you each time:

P – **Point**: Using the key words from the question, answer the question and make your point.

I – **Illustrate**: Select a quote or pick out something from an image to back up your point.

E – **Explain**: Tell the reader why you have picked the quote or the aspect from the image. Use your own personal opinion or experience to explain how it helps to answer the question.

Example – Ed Sheeran review answers

What impression do you get of Ed Sheeran from reading the review on pages 24–25?

> [P] I believe that Ed Sheeran is a clever and talented man.
>
> [I] He also uses family influences in tracks such as 'Galway Girl' …
>
> [E] Sheeran is very smart to write songs that appeal to a wide range of fans. The song 'Galway Girl' was written with his Irish fans in mind because he is so popular over here. By doing this, Sheeran is keeping all his fans happy. They also feel that they know him more because he shares a personal connection.

Practice makes perfect

This is an extract from *A Monster Calls* by Patrick Ness.

Sample extract

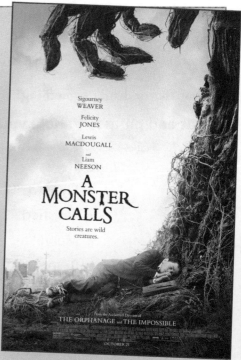

The monster showed up just after midnight. As they do.

Conor was awake when it came.

He'd had a nightmare. Well, not *a* nightmare. *The* nightmare. The one he'd been having a lot lately. The one with the darkness and the wind and the screaming. The one with the hands slipping from his grasp, no matter how hard he tried to hold on. The one that always ended with–

'Go away,' Conor whispered into the darkness of his bedroom, trying to push the nightmare back, not let it follow him into the world of waking. 'Go away now.'

He glanced over at the clock his mum had put on his bedside table. 12.07. Seven minutes past midnight. Which was late for a school night, late for a Sunday, certainly.

He'd told no one about the nightmare. Not his mum, obviously, but no one else either, not his dad in their fortnightly (or so) phone call, *definitely* not his grandma, and no one at school. Absolutely not.

What happened in the nightmare was something no one else ever needed to know.

Conor blinked groggily at his room, then he frowned. There was something he was missing. He sat up in his bed, waking a bit more. The nightmare was slipping from him, but there was something he couldn't put his finger on, something different, something–

He listened, straining against the silence, but all he could hear was the quiet house around him, the occasional tick from the empty downstairs or a rustle of bedding from his mum's room next door.

Nothing.

And then something. Something he realized was the thing that had woken him. Someone was calling his name.

Conor.

He felt a rush of panic, his guts twisting. Had it followed him? Had it somehow stepped out of the nightmare and–?

'Don't be stupid,' he told himself. 'You're too old for monsters.'

And he was. He'd turned thirteen just last month. Monsters were for babies. Monsters were for bed-wetters. Monsters were for–

Conor.

There it was again. Conor swallowed. It had been an unusually warm October, and his window was still open. Maybe the curtains shushing each other in the small breeze could have sounded like–

Conor.

All right, it wasn't the wind. It was definitely a voice, but not one he recognized. It wasn't his mother's, that was for sure. It wasn't a woman's voice at all, and he wondered for a crazy moment if his dad had somehow made a surprise trip from America and arrived too late to phone and–

Conor.

No. Not his dad. This voice had a quality to it, a *monstrous* quality, wild and untamed. Then he heard a heavy creak of wood outside, as if something gigantic was stepping across a timber floor.

He didn't want to go and look. But at the same time, a part of him wanted to look more than anything.

Sample questions and answers

Question 1   *5 marks*

True or False:

This was the first time Conor had this nightmare	F
The only person Conor told about his problems was his dad	F
His mother was sleeping next door	T
It was summer	F
His dad was on a trip to America	T

Allow 3 minutes for 5-mark questions.

Question 2   *20 marks*

1. Having read the text and examined the film poster on the previous page, describe whether you think the monster is scary or pleasant?

Allow 12 minutes for 20-mark questions.

Sample answer using PIE

[P] My impression of the monster is that he is pleasant. Having examined the poster, I believe he is a kind monster but just looks scary.

[I] In the image, it looks like he is giving his hand to the boy as if he is trying to be friendly. The colours in the background are orange and yellows, and this makes me think of being warm and safe.

[E] Personally, I'd say the monster looks and sounds scary but is actually quite nice in person.

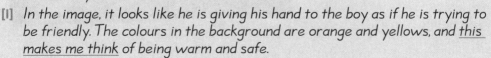

2. Do you think this sounds like an interesting story? Would you read on?

Sample answers using PIE

[P] *I feel that this story sounds like a very interesting one because I adore stories that have monsters in them.*

[I] *'Then he heard a heavy creak of wood outside, as if something gigantic was stepping across a timber floor.'*

[E] *Conor hears the monster but doesn't see him and he doesn't know where he is. This makes the extract quite scary to read because we don't know what is going to happen.*

[P] *I also would like to read on because Conor sounds like an interesting person.*

[I] *'He didn't want to go and look. But at the same time, a part of him wanted to look more than anything.'*

[E] *Conor is thirteen, and he is trying to be brave now that he is older. He tells himself 'Don't be stupid,' when he tries to convince himself to be brave. The fact that part of him wants to look at the monster shows us that he wants to try and face his fears.*

If you have the time, try and write two PIE paragraphs to achieve the best marks.

Practise your reading

The *Harry Potter: Hogwarts Mystery* Game – A Portkey to Hogwarts?

Sample review

A lot of people would die for the opportunity to spend a day at Hogwarts, meet all the characters and learn how to become a wizard. Well, here is your chance to meet Dumbledore, Hermione Granger and Ron Weasley with the new mobile game *Harry Potter: Hogwarts Mystery*. The game was released on 25 April 2018 to the excitement of Harry Potter fans. However, as a game, it had a lot to deliver to make players happy.

The game starts with an invitation from Dumbledore to begin your wizarding studies at Diagon Alley. While the graphics are basic, they do the job (they remind you of watching a cutsie version of the film). The game includes a lot of little things for fans such as voice-overs from the film's actors, references to hidden secrets and Harry Potter favourites such as the Sorting Hat.

Players are able to create their own character to walk around the magical world of Harry Potter. They can cast spells and create potions and find out who their friends and enemies are. However, problems occur very quickly if your character becomes entangled in a Devil's Snare and you run out of energy. At this point, the game will ask you to pay money in order to recharge your battery or you have the option to wait an hour.

Anyone who likes to play video games will not want to be stopped for an hour every time they become involved in a Devil's Snare. Asking players to wait for such a long time is a big downfall to this game. It certainly feels like a money-making scheme and fans of Harry Potter will find that they are frustrated at the game. It is hard to get through even a single wizarding class without tapping to see if you can go on or wait for the message to pay money.

Fans of Harry Potter are going to be very disappointed at this game as they will simply have to pay out a lot of money if they want continuous play. Even without the interruptions, the game becomes a little unexciting and boring. Once you have been to a couple of the lessons, they don't seem that exciting any more and even Harry Potter fans would lose interest. It's sad to say that *Harry Potter: Hogwarts Mystery* is no mystery; it is just not worth it.

Time to practise

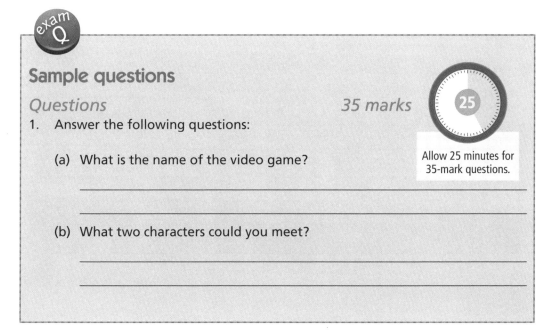

exam Q

Sample questions

Questions   *35 marks*   25

1.   Answer the following questions:

    (a) What is the name of the video game?

    Allow 25 minutes for 35-mark questions.

_____

_____

    (b) What two characters could you meet?

_____

_____

(c)   Name one place you go to study to become a wizard.

_____

_____

(d)   When was the game released?

_____

_____

(e)   Name two things that Harry Potter fans would like about this game.

_____

_____

2.   Do you think the writer liked the game? Write down two points and refer to the text when answering.

[P] _____

_____

[I] _____

_____

[E] _____

_____

_____

[P] _____

_____

[I] _____

_____

[E] _____

_____

_____

_____

3. Write the opening paragraph of a review based on a novel you have studied.

_____

_____

_____

_____

_____

_____

_____

_____

_____

_____

_____

exam focus

When writing the opening of a review, you must introduce the text and the name of its director/author/playwright. Your paragraph should give some idea of how you feel about the text and some background information.

exam Q

Exam Question (Junior Cycle 2018, Final Examination, English, Ordinary Level)

Section B – Reading and Responding Imaginatively

Read the following extract from Michael Morpurgo's short story, 'I Believe in Unicorns' and answer the questions.

My name is Tomas Porec. I was seven years old when I first met the unicorn lady. I believed in unicorns then. I am nearly twenty now and because of her I still believe in unicorns.

My little town, hidden deep in its own valley, was an ordinary place. But when I was seven it was a place of magic and wonder to me. I fished in the stream below the church, tobogganed the slopes in winter, swam in the lake in the summer.

I never did like school though. It wasn't the school's fault, nor the teachers'. I just wanted to be outside all the time. I longed always to be running free up in the hills. As soon as school was over, it was back home for some bread and honey – then off out to play. But one afternoon my mother had other ideas. She had to do some shopping in town, she said, and wanted me to go with her.

'I hate shopping,' I told her.

'I know that, dear,' she said. 'That's why I'm taking you to the library. It'll be interesting. It'll be good for you. There's a new librarian lady and she tells stories after school. Everyone says she's brilliant.' She walked me up the steps into the library. 'Be good,' she said, and she was gone.

I could see there was an excited huddle of children gathered in one corner. I noticed they were all jostling each other, as if they were desperate to get a better look at something. Suddenly they were all sitting down and hushed, and there in the corner I saw a unicorn. I could see now that he was made of carved wood and painted white, but he was so lifelike that if he'd got up and trotted off I wouldn't have been at all surprised.

Beside the unicorn and just as motionless, just as neat, stood a lady with a smiling face, a bright flowery scarf around her shoulders. When she sat down slowly on the unicorn and folded her hands in her lap I could feel expectation all around me.

'The unicorn story!' cried a little girl. 'Tell us the unicorn story. Please.'

She talked so softly that I had to lean forward to hear her. But I wanted to hear her, everyone did, because every word she spoke was meant and felt, and sounded true.

After she had finished no one spoke. Then a hand went up. It was a small boy from my school, Milos with the sticky-up hair. 'Can I tell a story, miss?' he asked. So sitting on the unicorn he told us his story. One after another after that they wanted their turn on the magical unicorn. I longed to have a go myself, but I didn't dare. I was frightened of making a fool of myself, I think. The hour flew by.

One afternoon the unicorn lady took out from her bag a rather old and damaged-looking book, all charred at the edges. It was, she told us, her very own copy of *The Little Match Girl* by Hans Christian Andersen. 'Why's it been burnt?' I asked her.

'This is the most precious book I have, Tomas,' she said. I'll tell you why. When I was very little I lived in another country. There were wicked people in my town who were frightened of the magic of stories and of the power of books, because stories make you think and dream; books make you want to ask questions. And they didn't want that. I was there with my father watching them burn a great pile of books, when suddenly my father ran forward and plucked a book out of the fire. The soldiers beat him with sticks, but he held on to the book and wouldn't let go of it. It was this book. It's my favourite book in all the world. Tomas, would you like to come and sit on the unicorn and read it to us?'

I had never been any good at reading out loud. But now, sitting on the magic unicorn, I heard my voice strong and loud. It was like singing a song. The words danced on the air and everyone listened.

Question 1   20 marks

Base your answers on the text printed on the previous page.
Place a tick ✓ in the box beside the correct answer. Tick one
box only in each case.

Allow 12 minutes for 20-mark questions.

(a) What age does the narrator Tomas tell the reader that he is
     now?

      Nineteen   ☐

      Twenty   ☐

      Twenty-one   ☐

      Thirty   ☐

(b) Why did Tomas not like school?

      He didn't like reading.   ☐

      He always wanted to be outside.   ☐

      He had no friends there.   ☐

      The teachers were not nice.   ☐

(c) Which of the following statements is false?

      Tomas's mother left him at the library because
      she thought it was good for him.   ☐

      Tomas's mother left him at the library because
      she wanted to go shopping.   ☐

      Tomas's mother left him at the library to
      do his homework.   ☐

      Tomas's mother left him at the library to
      hear the unicorn lady's stories.   ☐

(d) Why was Tomas frightened to read a story while sitting on the magic unicorn?

      He was scared of the unicorn lady.   ☐

      He was afraid of making a fool of himself.   ☐

      He thought that storytelling was just for younger children.   ☐

      He was too busy tobogganing.   ☐

Question 2   10 marks

Why do you think *The Little Match Girl* was the unicorn lady's
most precious book? Explain your answer.

Allow 6 minutes for 10-mark questions.

_____

_____

_____

_____
_____
_____
_____
_____
_____
_____
_____
_____
_____
_____

Cheat Sheet: Tips for successful reading and responding

You **must**:

1. **Read** the text and questions carefully ○
2. Use **PIE** ○
3. Be able to recognise each **style of writing** ○
4. Use correct **punctuation and grammar** ○

You **should**:

5. **Learn phrases** to help you **express your opinion** ○
6. Watch your **timing** ○
7. **Proofread** your answers ○

You **could**:

8. Learn **key vocabulary** to help you answer questions ○

It is really important when using PIE that you write as much as you can for your explanation. Aim for four or five sentences.

4 Writing for a Variety of Purposes

What does 'writing for a variety of purposes' mean?

As an English student, you must develop your ability to write for different reasons. You might have to write a personal letter to a friend, an email to an employer, a review of a computer game or even a short online message.

The following are some of the reasons we write:

To narrate

- To tell a story

Example – Extract from a short story

'Paul walked slowly through the corridor. He expected to see some students, but there was no one around. He approached his locker and opened it.'

To inform

- To provide useful or interesting information

Example – Extract from a news report

'The car was travelling at approximately 90 km/h when it struck the cyclist. The cyclist was rushed to Tallaght Hospital where her condition is described as critical but stable.'

To argue

- To use facts and evidence to prove a point

Example – Extract from a debate on gun control in the USA

Senator Kelly

David Todd

We cannot say that gun laws need to be stronger. People have a right to carry arms.

Senator Kelly, it is clear from recent history that gun laws need to be better. I'm just going to focus on school shootings. Between 2013 and 2015, 59 people were killed in shooting incidents at schools or colleges with another 124 injured, according to a recent report. These are supposed to be safe places not warzones, Senator.

To persuade

- To convince somebody of a particular point of view

Example – Extract from the script of an advertisement

DO YOU WANT TO RUN FASTER AND JUMP HIGHER?

Do you want comfort and support as you train?

The Cheetah Pumps are the most dynamic running shoe ever produced. Get yours today for just €109.99.

To analyse

- To examine something carefully to try and understand and explain it

Example – Extract from a programme on a Premier League football match in England

'Having looked at the two goals again, I think it's clear that Liverpool's defenders are not attacking crosses coming into the box. We can see two examples here, where the centre half has not jumped for the cross. The next clip shows the striker get above him and head home the first goal.'

To amuse

- To create something that will entertain or create laughter

Example – A joke

What did the fish say when he swam into the wall?

Dam!

To evaluate

- To decide, or attempt to decide, the value of something

Example – Extract from a job reference

<u>**Re: Job reference**</u>

Dear Human Resources Director,

Laura has been a vital part of this company. She has excellent communication and teamwork skills and shows a great ability to deal with challenges. She will be very difficult to replace.

To imagine

- To form a mental image of something that may not have been visualised or seen before

Example – Extract from a fantasy novel

Vaneas was one of the few mirror cities left in the world. A place where you could live two lives at once. You worked on one side and played on the other. As long as you never met your other self, the candle could burn forever.

To explore

- To inquire into or discuss a subject (often unfamiliar) in more detail

Example – An extract from a school project

I was excited to explore the geography, history and culture of France for this project. In the pages ahead, I will bring you on a journey through lots of things French. Hopefully by the end, you will have had as much fun as I had.

To engage

- To occupy someone's attention

Example – A poem

> *Friends hurt and blame.*
> *I hurt and blame.*
> *Data limit exceeded.*
> *Did they just say that?*
> *I hurt, I hurt, I hurt.*

Reader response: 'I love this poem. It reminds me of my own life and the stuff that goes on between friends.'

To explain

- To make something clear so that someone can understand it

Example – Extract from a science book

How is Food Digested?

- The food we eat is broken down and used by our bodies. This breaking down of food is called digestion.

- You may have heard your stomach gurgling after you have eaten. The stomach, teeth, tongue and intestines all help to digest food.

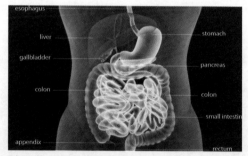

The digestive system

- When you chew your food, digestion begins. The food is pushed by the tongue to the trapdoor at the back of the mouth called the oesophagus.

- It then moves to the stomach where the digestive juices make it smaller. In the small intestine, the goodness is 'soaked up'. Finally, water is taken out in the large intestines.

- The goodness that is left can now be carried around the body by the blood, it is used for energy, repair and growth!

To criticise

- To form and express a judgement on a literary piece

Example – An extract from a review on *Grown Ups 2*

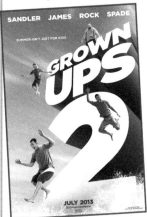

'I didn't enjoy the first film and I cannot advise people enough against the second instalment. The jokes are old, lazy and, in most cases, insulting, the characters have nothing to them and I'm still wondering how Adam Sandler has ended up in another bad movie.'

To comment

- To give a short response to or opinion on something

Example – A tweet responding to a story about Facebook

Totes Shocked @too_shocked Nov 27

I'm done with Facebook. I can't trust them to protect my private data. #distrust #bigbrother

Time to practise

Can you think of three writing purposes for each of the following texts?

- Diary
- Speech
- Email
- Letter
- Blog
- Review
- Social media post
- Article

As you have seen, people write for lots of different purposes. For example, a review could be used to inform, criticise and evaluate. You must practise the different forms in order to improve.

key point

By reading and writing in different forms and genres, you will build skills and develop the ability to write for a **variety of purposes**.

You will write for a **variety of purposes** when completing your portfolio. This experience, along with your ongoing class work and homework, will give you the skills you need for your final exam. You will understand the success criteria that go with different pieces of work.

Following the **RAFT** structure is very helpful when preparing to write something.

RAFT GUIDELINES

ROLE OF THE WRITER

Who am I as the writer? What is my personality? How will I react to information or a situation? My role depends on the situation; for example, am I a film critic writing a review, or a customer writing a letter of complaint?

AUDIENCE

For whom am I writing? Who needs to read this? Who am I trying to persuade? What is the goal or purpose of writing? What type of emotional reaction do I want from the reader?

FORMAT

In what format am I writing? There are numerous possibilities, for example, an article, a diary entry, a speech, an opinion piece.

TOPIC

What am I writing about? What is the subject I am covering? What information do I have to share? What is the focus of my chosen format?

Success criteria for written pieces – samples

The following samples are accompanied by **success criteria**. You are told what you **must**, what you **should** and what you **could do** in order for your piece to be successful. For **guidance**, we will show you where the 'I must ...' occurs in each piece.

Diary entry

A **diary entry** is a personal piece of writing where someone reveals their inner thoughts. It is private and honest and is usually written in an **informal** way.

Example – Jen's diary entry

1 ➤ 10/08/2018

Dear Lotty, ➤ **2**

5 ➤ I'm so angry right now, I could eat this pen! Sarah is now –
3 ➤ according to TJ – my 'ex-friend'. I mean, why is she making
such a big deal about this? I know she's angry about
Gary going out with me instead of her, but that's not my
4 ➤ problem. Why can't she just be supportive? It was okay
for her to date Cian when she knew I liked him. TJ said
she's saying stuff about me on Facebook, but I can't see it
because my cruel Mum took my stupid computer. I don't
even want to get started on Mum. Everything is so unfair.
I'll pick this up later – when I'm calmer …

Jen

Cheat Sheet: Success criteria for writing diary entries

You **must**:
1. Write the **date above** each entry
2. Write in the **first person** using the personal pronoun '**I**'
3. **Narrate events** that have happened
4. **Comment** on the **events** you describe
5. Show **emotions**

You **should**:
6. Use **descriptive** language
7. Write in an **informal** style

You **could**:
8. Think of the diary **as a character** and give them a **name**

Time to practise

Write a diary entry about a positive experience you had involving one of your pastimes/hobbies. Use the success criteria shown above to help you.

Review

The purpose of a review is to tell others about an experience. Traditionally, reviews were printed in magazines and newspapers. Now, they also appear on radio and television and, most commonly, on the internet.

Example: Review of the film, *Wonder*

1 *Wonder* **fills the big screen with hope and love.**

As I walked from the movie theatre, I couldn't help but feel uplifted. *Wonder*, directed by Stephen Chbosky, is the **2** feel-good movie of 2017. It pulls at the heart strings and strengthens your spirit.

3 August Pullman is a ten-year-old boy starting middle school in Beecher Prep. But he's not just any kid. He has Treacher Collins syndrome, a condition that has left him with a severe facial deformity. He is also starting school for the first time. The author, R.J. Palacio, brings us on a wonderful adventure through the eyes of August, his family and friends.

He must figure out who his friends really are and characters like Jack Will, Summer and Julian must all go through their own journeys. His sister, Via, must meet the challenges of high school and the painful distance between her and her best friend, Miranda. The beauty of this story is that August is central to all of this and as Via says, 'August is the sun.'

4 August isn't likeable straight away. I found him a bit needy at first, but when I thought about what he had to go through, I really began to have sympathy for him. Jack Will is a great character because there are so many kids who just want to do the right thing but inevitably mess up.

5 Having read the book I was disappointed that so many little things were changed. I mean August showing up to school in his astronaut helmet was just silly. However, the character of Justin was far more likeable in the film.

If you haven't seen it yet, you need to book your ticket today. Palacio created a story that everyone can relate to while dealing with issues that are really serious in a fun fashion. The film wasn't just like the book, but the message is the same. Everyone is someone.
Star rating: 5 stars.

Cheat Sheet: Success criteria for writing reviews

You **must**:

1. Include the **title** of what you are reviewing, i.e. a book, film, video game, etc. ○

2. Mention who **wrote/directed/designed** it ○

3. Give a brief **summary** of the content ○

4. Give your **opinion** on three or four aspects of it ○

5. Use **paragraphs** ○

You **should**:

6. Follow the **RAFT** structure ○

7. Suggest things you would **change** about the item ○

8. Say if you would **recommend** it to others ○

9. Give it a **star rating** ○

You **could**:

10. **Compare** this with other **similar genres** ○

Time to practise

Write a review of one of the following. Use the success criteria shown above to help you.

- A film or TV show you have watched recently
- A novel or short story you have read
- A video game you have played
- A music album you have listened to.

Informal letter

An informal letter is written to someone you know. It usually gives details of personal events or opinions.

Example – Charlie's letter

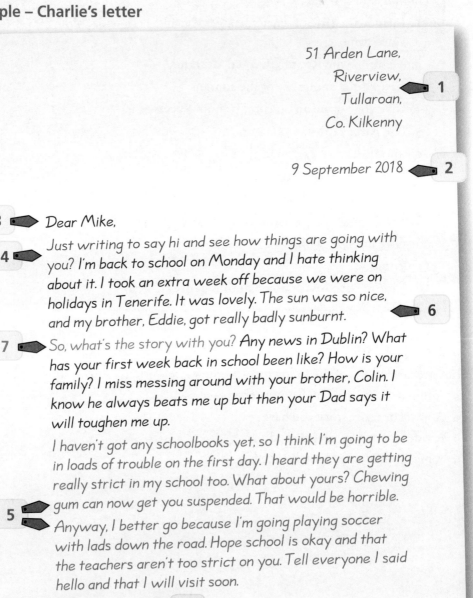

51 Arden Lane,
Riverview,
Tullaroan,
Co. Kilkenny
1

9 September 2018 **2**

3 Dear Mike,

4 Just writing to say hi and see how things are going with you? I'm back to school on Monday and I hate thinking about it. I took an extra week off because we were on holidays in Tenerife. It was lovely. The sun was so nice, and my brother, Eddie, got really badly sunburnt. **6**

7 So, what's the story with you? Any news in Dublin? What has your first week back in school been like? How is your family? I miss messing around with your brother, Colin. I know he always beats me up but then your Dad says it will toughen me up.

I haven't got any schoolbooks yet, so I think I'm going to be in loads of trouble on the first day. I heard they are getting really strict in my school too. What about yours? Chewing gum can now get you suspended. That would be horrible.

5 Anyway, I better go because I'm going playing soccer with lads down the road. Hope school is okay and that the teachers aren't too strict on you. Tell everyone I said hello and that I will visit soon.

See you soon, **8**

Charlie

Cheat Sheet: Success criteria for writing informal letters

You **must**:

1. Write your **address** in the top **right-hand corner** ○
2. Write the **date** just below the address ○
3. Open your letter with **a greeting** (for example, 'Dear John', 'Hi Clare') ○
4. Use the **first line to explain** why you are writing ○
5. Use **paragraphs** ○
6. Give **information** ○
7. Ask **questions** ○
8. **Sign off** (for example, 'Best wishes', 'Take care', 'See you soon') ○

You **should**:

9. Use a **variety of verbs**, **adjectives** and **adverbs** to express your point ○

Time to practise

Write an informal letter to a friend in a different country where you describe your summer holidays. Use the success criteria shown above to help you.

Speech

A speech is an opinion piece that is spoken to an audience.

Motion
A statement that people argue for or against.

key words

Example – Speech to a school assembly

Write a speech that you would perform to your school assembly of students, teachers and parents for or against the motion: Teenagers should be called 'screenagers' because they are addicted to screens – TV, phones, electronic games, and so on.

1 Ladies and gentlemen,

I am speaking today because I believe teenagers should not **2** be called 'screenagers'. Teenagers are not addicted to screens even though some adults think this is the case. Technology is an important part of our lives, but there is much more to us than the technology we use.

Addicted is a very strong word. It means you can't give something up. Personally, I could survive a week without seeing a screen. There's nothing good on most of the time, anyway. There are lots of things young people do that have nothing to do with screens. When you call us 'screenagers', it makes us sound like zombies who have no control.

4 I like Facebook and TV. I like chatting with my friends, but only when I've done my chores around the house and completed my homework. My mum doesn't think it's a good idea to spend too long watching TV, and I agree because it hurts your eyes. My friends are the same, so to call us all 'screenagers' is wrong. The other day one of my friends **5** suggested we play *FIFA*, but we told him that we wanted to play real football outside instead.

Teenagers are interested in lots of things that have nothing **3** to do with screens. We play sport and go for walks. We meet **7** our friends and chat. We don't all just gather around a TV for hours and refuse to talk. Recent research showed that 55 per cent of teenagers spend less time on their screens **6** than their parents or other adults in their lives.

I think adults are scared of young people on screens because they don't know what we are doing all the time. Can you ask us? Of course, you can. Can you learn something? Definitely. I was able to show my dad how to change something for a work project. You need to trust us. You need to see that this can be a good thing.

Adults often spend as much time looking at screens as young people and sometimes more because a lot of them work in offices. I know teenagers are anything but 'screenagers'.

Thank you.

Cheat Sheet: Success criteria for writing speeches

You **must**:

1. **Address** the audience
2. Share your **point of view respectfully**
3. Include **accurate information** about the topic you are speaking about
4. Use **paragraphs to divide** your points

You **should**:

5. Use **anecdotes** (This is a short, personal story to highlight a point you are making.)
6. Use **statistics to support** your arguments
7. Use **repetition to emphasise** a point

You **could**:

8. Use **humour**
9. Include **quotes** to support a point

Time to practise

Write a speech to persuade a group of young people why sport and exercise is important.

Blog post

Blog is short for 'web log'. It is a journal that is written online. Blog writers (bloggers) discuss topics personal to them or share their opinions on issues they think are important.

Example – Blog post on exam stress

1

DON'T STRESS ABOUT THE JUNIOR CYCLE EXAMS!

My friends have been talking a lot this week about our exams. It's making me ill. Every time I turn around someone is freaking about German or Science or English. I say – what's **3** the point? Don't get me wrong, I'm concerned about my exams and I really want to do well. I see their importance for me next year, but stress is not in my vocabulary.

I've done some work in some subjects; I've done a lot in others. And I'm not going to lie – I haven't looked at Geography. It just got pushed down the list of priorities. Not a good idea for anyone preparing for exams.

You're probably wondering why I'm not getting stressed if I have so much work to do. Well, firstly, this is not the Hunger Games. I'm not going to die if I'm not up to the standard. It's a really important exam, but the sun will still be up in **2** the morning and I'll still have to go to school in September – AGAIN!

Secondly, if you don't get what you want in your exams or they don't go to plan, you can make another plan. My mum always told me that the best thing about life is that you can keep hitting the reset button and start again. So, I'm going to try my best in these exams and whatever will be, will be. I'll still have my friends and family to support me.

4 If you have worked really hard and are worried you won't get the results you want, please remember there is a reason for everything. Sometimes the path you think is right just isn't for you. Everyone finds their path eventually. I'm going to find mine, now … any minute now … well, maybe I'll wait a little longer.

My advice is to do your best. Attempt everything, and when you finish the exams, go do something fun with your family or friends. It'll be all okay in the end.

See you next week when I'll be investigating my friend's social media addiction. I'll also update you on my exams.

STRESS!

5

Cheat Sheet: Success criteria for writing blog posts

You **must**:

1. Include a **headline** ◯
2. Give your **opinion** ◯
3. Write in **the first person** ◯
4. Use **paragraphs** ◯
5. Provide an **image** ◯
6. Use accurate **spelling and grammar** ◯

You **should**:

7. **Experiment** with different vocabulary ◯
8. **Research** your topic well ◯
9. Use the **RAFT** structure ◯

You **could**:

10. **Design** the blog page ◯
11. Write **multiple entries** to complement the piece ◯
12. **Publish** it online ◯

Time to practise

Write a blog post where you talk about the challenges young people face in today's world.

Email

Email stands for electronic mail. This is an online message, very like a letter. Emails can be **formal** or **informal**.

Emails are completed electronically but if you are asked to write one out you must include an email address, date and subject as you will see in the template below.

Example – Formal email

The following **formal** email was written by a customer to their TV provider to complain about poor service.

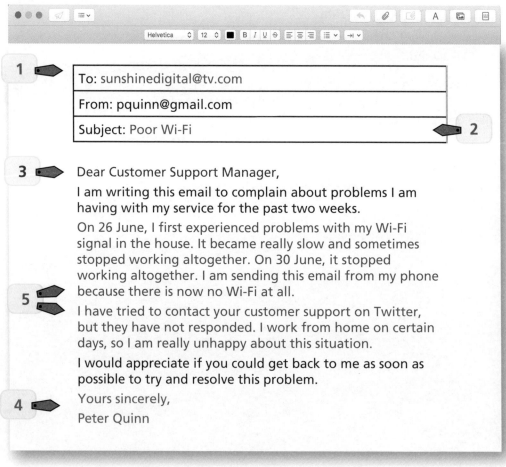

1 → To: sunshinedigital@tv.com

From: pquinn@gmail.com

Subject: Poor Wi-Fi ← **2**

3 → Dear Customer Support Manager,

I am writing this email to complain about problems I am having with my service for the past two weeks.

On 26 June, I first experienced problems with my Wi-Fi signal in the house. It became really slow and sometimes stopped working altogether. On 30 June, it stopped working altogether. I am sending this email from my phone

5 → because there is now no Wi-Fi at all.

I have tried to contact your customer support on Twitter, but they have not responded. I work from home on certain days, so I am really unhappy about this situation.

I would appreciate if you could get back to me as soon as possible to try and resolve this problem.

4 → Yours sincerely,

Peter Quinn

Cheat Sheet: Success criteria for writing emails

You **must**:

1. Insert the **email address** of the person you are writing to in the **address** bar ○
2. Write a **short note** in the **subject bar** to show what the email is about ○
3. Start your email with an **appropriate greeting** ○
4. Finish your email with an **appropriate sign-off** ○
5. Use **paragraphs** ○
6. Use **correct punctuation and grammar** ○

You **should**:

7. Be respectful and courteous ○
8. Use the **RAFT** structure ○
9. Include **quotes** to support a point ○

key words

Appropriate
Means suitable or correct in a particular situation. For example, you wouldn't say 'Yo Bro!' in an email to your school principal.

Time to practise

Imagine you are a member of the Student Council in your school. Write a formal email to your principal where you outline some ideas you have to improve the school.

Short story

Short stories are pieces of creative writing with a setting, plot, characters and dramatic moments.

Example – Short mystery story

The following is the opening paragraph to a short mystery story.

1 ➤ Jenna crept from her room and tiptoed to the top of the wooden stairs. She could hear soft whispering downstairs, and a small beam of light came from under the kitchen door. She pushed open her parents' door and saw that they were sound asleep. A shiver ran down her spine as she realised that someone else was in the house. What was she going to do?

She sat on the top step and strained her ears to hear what was being said downstairs.

'This is our house. The visitors must go.'

Jenna jumped up and banged her elbow against the banisters. Immediately, the light went out and the whispering stopped.

3 ➤ Jenna hadn't wanted to move to Cedar Falls. They had moved because of her mum's job. She was an archaeologist and was working on a dig near an old church. They had moved into a house just a mile from the site. All the houses around it were broken down, but theirs was perfect with beautiful ◄ **2** white walls and spotlessly clean windows. Inside was weirdly the same, considering no one had lived there for ten years. The only cobwebs were the ones over the cellar door. It was locked, and her dad had spent all week looking for a key.

Cheat Sheet: Success criteria for writing short stories

You **must**:

1. **Grab the reader's attention** with an interesting opening paragraph ◯
2. Create an **interesting setting** ◯
3. **Develop one or two characters** in detail ◯
4. **Build the action** to a **climax** ◯
5. Bring your story to a **satisfying conclusion** ◯

You **should**:

6. Include other **minor characters** ◯
7. Use a **variety of descriptive verbs, adverbs and adjectives** ◯
8. Use paragraphs ◯
9. Include **direct speech** ◯

Climax
The highest point of drama or action in a story.

You are more likely to write short stories for CBA 2, but you might be asked to write an opening paragraph or a descriptive paragraph in your final exam.

Drama script

A drama script is the written text of a play.

Example – Drama script extract from *Grave Expectations*

The following is an extract from a play about a gentle teacher's struggles in a school in the 1960s.

5 ➤ Grave Expectations

6 ➤ *Scene: A classroom.*

There are two rows of four tables facing stage right. There is a fireplace on the stage-left wall. Several hurleys line the back wall. Mr Reilly, the teacher, enters with a small brown satchel under his left arm and a hurley in his right hand. Five boys eagerly sit upright as he enters. A sixth boy, Kevin Flynn, sits on his desk.

1 ➤ Mr Reilly: Get down off that table, Flynn, and grab the turf.

Kevin: *[grinning]* I've a sore back, sir.

2 Mr Reilly: If ya sat properly on your chair, you wouldn't have any of that bother. Don't give me any nonsense. A young lad like you. Grab the turf, and we'll try bring a little heat to the dungeon. **4**

Kevin: I think we'll need more than turf to heat this place.

[laughter]

Mr Reilly: Quiet, boys. We're not at the funfair.

[Kevin hops down and moves to the fireplace. He takes two sods of turf and stacks them in the fire.] **3**

Kevin: There's no matches.

Mr Reilly: Rooney, did you bring the matches?

Rooney: No, sir. My mother couldn't spare them.

Mr Reilly: Well, lads, looks like we'll have to go outside for a few pucks to get warmed up.

[The boys jump up excitedly and run to grab the hurleys.] **3**

Mr Dunne: *[speaking in a deep voice from the door]* What is going on here, Mr Reilly?

Mr Reilly: No turf, Tom. We said we'd go for a puck and get warmed up.

Mr Dunne: A few pucks is it? What about arithmetic at nine o'clock, or are you teaching some new curriculum the rest of us don't know about? Get back to your seats, boys. As long as your brains are warm, we'll not worry too much about the rest of ye. And, Reilly, you'll refer to me as Mr Dunne in front of these boys. It's bad enough that their parents don't teach them any manners. We have to keep them in check.

Cheat Sheet: Success criteria for writing drama

You **must**:

1. Place the name of the **character speaking** on the **left-hand side** of the page before their line ○
2. Go to a **new line** every time the **speaker changes** ○
3. Include **stage directions** to show what the characters are doing ○
4. Create **a connection and/or conflict** between the characters that will **entertain** your audience ○

You **should**:

5. Give your piece a **title** ○
6. Give a **brief introduction of the setting** and background to the scene ○

key point

Sometimes you may be asked to write a piece of dialogue in the exam, and this is similar to a drama script.

key words

Stage Directions
Instructions for the actors that show how a line is to be read or what the character is doing.

5 Appreciating Visual and Digital Genres

 I will learn how to:

- Identify, understand and respond to different types of visual and digital texts
- Describe images
- Write about creating these texts

- What is a visual text? This is where an image or picture has a strong place on the page.
- What is a digital text? This is anything that has electronic or digital content.
- When you are studying visual and digital texts, you will find similarities between the two categories.

Some examples of visual and digital texts

Visual	*Digital*
• Posters	• Blogs
• Photographs	• Radio talks
• Camera shots	• Radio or film documentary
• Video game covers	• Film
• Advertisements	• Animation
• Infographics	• Web pages
• Cartoons	
• Brochures	
• Web pages	

Even though radio doesn't include any visuals, we still call it a digital text.

Understanding visual and digital texts

- **Posters** – People make posters to:
  - advertise a service or product – for example, a book
  - highlight important issues – for example, bullying
  - protest – for example, 'End Homelessness Now!'
  - celebrate something – for example, the anniversary of the 1916 Easter Rising.
- **Camera shots** – Photographers or film crew use different shots to capture a particular mood or message.
- **Video game covers** – These are the images and words on the front of the video game box or packaging. They are arranged in a special way to make the product look attractive and exciting. The cover can also provide information about the game, for example, the age certificate, the name and what the game is about.
- **Advertisements** – Adverts are used to encourage people to buy a product or services. They usually use a combination of images, words, music, dialogue and storytelling.
- **Infographic** – An infographic uses a combination of words, numbers and images in a special way to get its point across.
- **Cartoons** – Cartoons use images to show the cartoonist's interpretation or opinion of something. Cartoons usually feature words or dialogue.
- **Brochures** – Brochures are small books that provide information about a product or service. They use a mixture and variety of words, numbers and images.
- **Web pages** – Web pages have individual layouts that use a combination of headings, sub-headings, images, words, numbers, links, interactive images, audio and video clips.

How to read a visual text

Ask yourself these questions whenever you look at a visual text:

- Who or what is in the image?
- What is happening?
- Is there anything in the background?
- Are the colours important?
- If there are people, what are they wearing?
- Is there anything unusual about the lighting?
- Are there any words?
- What do you think the message is?

key point

You will be asked to study these visual texts and talk about them. You must be able to read a visual text and look out for important clues about the message it is trying to suggest.

exam focus

Sometimes the exam questions won't ask you for all of this detail. However, if it suits the question, you can add some of it in, as long as you make sure you answer the question. **Answering the question** is the most important thing to do.

Example – Reading a visual text

These are things you may have noticed when looking at or reading the image on the right:

- There are three teenagers: two boys and one girl.
- They are looking up at something and they look worried.
- In the background, there are tree trunks, so it looks like they are in a forest.
- The teenagers are wearing bright clothes which are very different to their dark brown and green surroundings.
- Their clothes are casual, and they don't have any jackets on. It seems like they were not planning on being there.
- The lighting is dark in the background, but the teenagers are brighter. The lighting makes it look like a very scary place.
- There are no words.
- I think the message in this picture is that they are in danger or are scared of something.

exam focus

When you are in your exam, don't miss out on any of the small print (writing). Make sure you read all of the words in the text.

Exam Question 2017 (SEC Junior Cycle Sample 1)

Study the still pictures taken from the film *Song of the Sea*. Still pictures are pictures taken from a film where the action is frozen. Complete the tasks that follow.

Question and sample answer   *10 marks*

Based on what you can see in the still pictures 1–4 on the previous page, write a paragraph that starts with one of the following prompts:

The pictures made me think that the film is **humorous** because ...

Allow 6 minutes for 10-mark questions.

or

The pictures made me think that the film is **imaginative** because ...

Fill in the blank and continue with your choice.

The pictures made me think that the film is _____*imaginative*_____ because ...

There are lots of unusual things in the film stills. In the first image, we can see that it is a girl's birthday, and it looks like she is wishing for something. In the second still, it is hard to make out what is going on. This image is mainly blue, but it looks like something magical is happening, and it seems as if her wish might come true. In the third still, the brother is trying to take away something from the girl. It looks like a giant snail; this is strange so I'm guessing it is something magical. In the fourth still, it looks as though the girl is flying. There are three birds around her carrying her off somewhere. This is why I think it is imaginative because it looks like the film is about magic.

How to read visual texts with words

Some visual texts will have an image, but they will also have words. You must read the information very carefully, but you must also study the image to understand the text fully. Sometimes, the words and information will have an important link to the image.

Ask yourself these questions when reading a visual text with words:

Study the image on the following page using the questions listed below:

- Is there a product being sold?
- Where do you see words on the page?
- Are the words in colour or in a particular font?
- Are there any persuasive words?
- Are there any brands or logos?
- Are there any numbers?
- Is anyone talking?

These are things you may have noticed when looking at or reading this poster advertising the Disney cartoon, *Moana*.

There is a young girl, a big man, a pig and a hen. They are animated characters.

The main characters look brave and strong. The girl is holding an oar. The man is holding a giant fish hook. They are standing on sand, surrounded by big, blue waves. It looks like they are on an exciting adventure.

In the background there are huge bright blue waves with many types of colourful sea creatures in them. The sky is blue with a few clouds. There are mountains and palm trees in the distance.

The writing at the bottom of the poster tells you the date the film will come out in cinemas. There are also numbers underneath the film title explaining that you can see the film in 2D or 3D.

The characters are wearing tribal outfits, which suggests they're from somewhere warm, far away and exotic. The man is covered in tribal tattoos.

The main actors are listed at the top and the movie title is at the bottom of the page.

This is a really colourful and exciting poster. It looks like the wind is whipping up around the characters and the waves look like they are parting around them as if by magic.

The brand is Disney.

The product is the film *Moana*.

There is writing at the bottom and top of the page in different fonts, colours and sizes.

Exam Question 2018 (Junior Cycle 2018, Final Examination, English, Ordinary Level)

ENJOY FREEDOM

Section C – Writing for a variety of purposes

Question   *10 marks*

1. Study the advertisement for camping equipment shown above. Why do you think the phrase *ENJOY FREEDOM* is used in this advertisement? Explain your answer.

Allow 6 minutes for 10-mark questions.

How to read a digital text

Ask yourself these questions when reading a digital text:

- What type of digital text is it?
- What is the layout?
- Are there any words?
- Are there any visuals?
- What is the purpose of the digital text?
- Are there any links?
- Are there any videos?
- Are people speaking?
- Is there any music?
- Are there any sound effects?

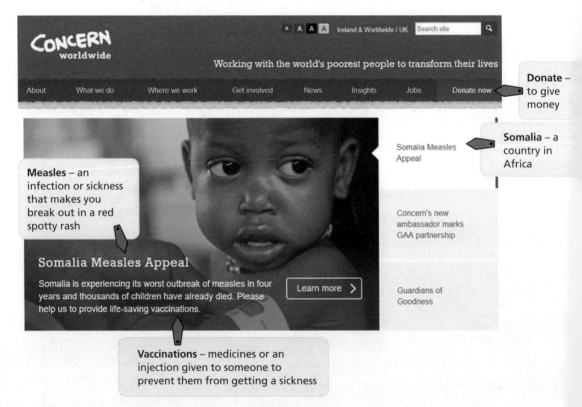

These are things you may have noticed when looking at or reading the above web page:

- This is a web page/website.
- The layout has a green banner with the company's **logo**, Concern Worldwide, on the left. Across the rest of the banner, there is a **search bar** and **tagline**: 'Working with the world's poorest people to help them transform their lives.' There are a

number of tabs and the pink one says 'Donate now'. Underneath, there is a large **image** of a baby being vaccinated. There is information on the picture about the Somalia measles appeal and how donating money can help provide life-saving vaccinations.

- There is a lot of information on this page, but it is divided up so it is easy to read. It also gives an opportunity to click on links to the part you want to see.
- The visual eye-catching and appeals to our emotions as the child in the photo is very young with big eyes and a worried expression.
- There are links to other parts of the website.
- There are no videos.
- No one is speaking.
- There is no music.
- There are no sound effects.

How to read an advertisement

Advertisements contain words and visuals, but they also have special features that you must be aware of.

Ask yourself these questions when reading an advertisement:

- What is the product (the item that they are selling, e.g. runners, milk, video games)?
- Who is the target audience (the people the advert is aimed at)?
- Is there any catchphrase or slogan?
- Are there any buzzwords (words that make the product sound appealing, e.g. creamy, refreshing, comfortable, etc.)?
- Is there repetition (repeated words or numbers)?
- Is there any copy (text that gives information about the product)?
- What colours are used?
- Are there are special effects, music or editing?

exam focus

Remember, advertisements want to sell something, so most exam questions will want you to think about who they are selling it to and whether the advertisement is good or bad.

exam Q

Sample questions and answers

 20

Questions   *30 marks*

Examine the following infographic and answer the
questions below:

Allow 20 minutes for
30-mark questions.

MINDS ◯ MATTER
THE TRUTH ON CONCUSSIONS

What are the Symptoms of a Concussion?

 key words

PHYSICAL

✓ Headache
✓ Nausea and vomiting
✓ Balance problems
✓ Slowed reaction time
✓ Dizziness
✓ Sensitivity to light
✓ Sensitivity to sound
✓ Fuzzy or blurry vision

Concussion
An injury to
the brain.

SLEEP

✓ Sleeping more or less than usual
✓ Trouble falling asleep
✓ Feeling fatigued or drowsy

Z Z Z

✓ Difficulty concentrating
✓ Difficulty remembering
✓ Confusion
✓ Feeling "mentally foggy"
✓ Feeling slowed down

THINKING AND REMEMBERING

MOOD DISRUPTION

✓ More emotional
✓ Irritable
✓ Sad
✓ Nervous
✓ Depressed

GH The Children's Hospital
of Philadelphia®

For more information visit: www.chop.edu/concussion
©2013 The Children's Hospital of Philadelphia. All Rights Reserved

1. Please tick the best option:
   (1) The poster is divided into how many main points?
      A. 6 ☐
      B. 2 ☐
      C. 4 ✔
   (2) In the section on 'Mood Disruption', what kind of emotions do you see on the faces?
      A. Happy and sad ☐
      B. Sad and angry ✔
      C. Happy and angry ☐
   (3) Who is responsible for making this poster?
      A. The Children's Hospital of Philadelphia ✔
      B. Chop Education ☐
      C. Mind Matters ☐
   (4) How would you best describe the theme of this infographic?
      A. Education ☐
      B. Health ✔
      C. Sport ☐

2. Infographics use a mixture of text and pictures to put across a message. Do you like this way of getting messages? Explain your answer.

   [P] *I believe that using infographics is helpful to put across a message because the information is clear.*

   [I] *'Mood Disruption – irritable, sad, nervous.'*

   [E] *This tells us the main things that can happen to your mood if you get concussion. It uses key words instead of lots of text, so it makes it easier to read and remember.*

   [P] *Each section also has a picture to help us to think of the main point.*

   [I] *In the pink 'Physical' section, it has a picture of a brain inside a head.*

   [E] *This is good because you remember the word 'Physical' more because it has the head and brain to go with it.*

3. Imagine you had to design an infographic to highlight bullying. Explain why you think bullying is such an important topic to talk about.

   Bullying is really important to talk about because it is so common these days. Bullying can hurt people and make them feel terrible. It is important to talk about it, so people stop doing it and for people to understand that if they are being bullied, they should go and talk to someone. People can be bullied for lots of different reasons, so it affects many teenagers today.

   Online bullying is used a lot, and it is very hard to stop it because people can hide behind a screen. These bullies can say anything, and they are not blamed because no one knows who they are. Teenagers need to know about the dangers of going online, but they also need to know who they can go to if they find themselves being bullied.

Sample questions

Questions   *30 marks*

Examine the following film poster and answer the questions that follow:

Allow 20 minutes for 30-mark questions.

1. Answer the following questions:

   (a) When is the film going to be in cinemas?

   _____

   (b) Name one actor listed on the poster.

   _____

   (c) Describe the main character's costume.

   _____
   _____
   _____
   _____

(d) Where do you think this film is set? Explain your answer with reference to the image.

_____

_____

_____

(e) Describe the lighting in the background of the poster. Explain why you think it looks like this.

_____

_____

_____

(f) Imagine you are designing a poster for the film you have studied. Describe what it would look like.

_____

_____

_____

_____

_____

_____

_____

2. You have been given the task of directing an actor in a key scene from your film. Tell the actor about the character he/she is going to play and what they should do to play the part.

You should:

- Describe what is going on in the key scene
- Describe the character's personality
- Give advice to the actor about their use of movement, voice and facial expression.

Name of film: _____

Director: _____

_____

_____

_____

_____

Sample questions

Questions   *25 marks*

Examine the following advertisement and answer the
questions that follow:

Allow 15 minutes for
25-mark questions.

1. True or False:

   (a) The product is Cheerios cereal

   (b) The product is aimed at children

   (c) There are no buzzwords in this advertisement

   (d) The slogan is 'Wake up to nutella'

   (e) There are 50 hazelnuts in every jar

2. Who do you think this advertisement is aimed at, parents or children? Explain
    your answer.

    _____

    _____

    _____

    _____

    _____

3. Do you think the advertisement is trying to say that Nutella is healthy? Give
    reasons for your answer.

    _____

    _____

    _____

    _____

    _____

4. Answer the following questions:

    (a) Imagine you were in charge of advertising fruity yoghurts. Who would be
        the age group you would sell it to (target audience)? Explain your answer.

        _____

        _____

        _____

        _____

    (b) List three buzzwords (words that make the product sound good) that you
        would use to advertise them.

        _____

        _____

        _____

        _____

    (c) Write a slogan/catchphrase for your product.

        _____

        _____

        _____

        _____

6 Novel

aims I will learn to:

- Discuss important characters and relationships
- Identify themes and literary techniques
- Explore key moments
- Compare two novels

Understanding characters

Understanding a character's personality and motives (why they do things) is a really important way to examine a novel. The main character is also the **protagonist** and often the villain can be called the **antagonist**.

Here are some questions to help you really understand your main character:

> **How would you describe your character in three words?**
>
> **Where are they from?**
>
> **What age are they?**
>
> **What problems do they have?**
>
> **Do they have any hopes or dreams?**
>
> **Describe the important relationships in their life.**

Example of understanding a character – Batman

Three adjectives I would choose to describe Batman are **moody, dark** and **heroic**. Batman is from **Gotham**. This is an imaginary place where there is a lot of crime and problems in the city. Batman ends up fighting criminals because he doesn't want to live in a city where there is so much evil. He also has a **problem in keeping his superhero powers secret from anyone else**. Batman is in his **late twenties or thirties**, but he seems to be very serious for his age. He hopes that Gotham will be a nicer place. Batman doesn't have any family. He is an orphan, but he has a great relationship with his butler, Alfred. Alfred is like a father to him. Batman would also like to have a romantic relationship with a woman, but he can't because he feels he always needs to protect them from danger.

Types of relationships

All characters are involved in some type of relationship, and it is up to you to discuss the types of relationships they are in.

1. Romantic
2. Friendship
3. Family
4. Professional
5. Community

Words to help you describe relationships:

- Love
- Hate
- Passion
- Fear
- Marriage
- Respect/disrespect
- Jealousy

- Loyal
- Caring
- Helpful
- Protection
- Complicated (difficult)
- Dysfunctional (not acting normal)

Examples

1. *Of Mice and Men* by John Steinbeck
   George and Lennie have been **friends** for years and are very **loyal** to each other. Even though George often gets fed up with Lennie, he still looks out for him. Their **friendship** is very special, and George stays **loyal** to Lennie even when things go badly wrong and George is faced with some hard decisions.

2. *Noughts & Crosses* by Malorie Blackman
   Calum and Sephy are **friends** at the beginning of the story, but their relationship changes to a **romantic** one. Their relationship is **complicated** because Sephy is a Nought (a black person) and Calum is a Cross (a white person), and they are not allowed to be together because of their race. They love each other, but the place where they live doesn't allow Noughts and Crosses to be together.

3. *Chalkline* by Jane Mitchell
   Jameela's brother, Rafiq, is kidnapped by rebels when he is nine and Jameela and her mother never give up hope of finding him. However, Jameela's father doesn't want to look for his son. This makes Jameela's family life very **complicated**. But Jameela doesn't give up hope and remains **loyal** to her brother.

Cinderella – key moments for her character and relationships

key point

Characters and their relationships can often go on a journey and end up in a very different place. It is important to map this journey in your own studied novel and pick out key moments where the characters or relationships change.

KEY MOMENT 1: Cinderella was a very happy girl who lived with her father. She was a caring and helpful person who loved her father very much. Her father remarried, and Cinderella got a new stepmother and two stepsisters.

KEY MOMENT 2: When Cinderella's father died, her life began to change for the worse. Her stepmother and stepsisters were very mean to her and made her do all the housework. However, Cinderella stayed true to her caring and helpful personality and did the work without complaint.

KEY MOMENT 3: Things changed when the whole family were invited to a ball at the king's palace, but Cinderella's new family wouldn't let her go with them. A fairy godmother helped her out and used magic to make her a new dress, carriage and servants.

KEY MOMENT 4: Cinderella went to the ball and met the prince. He danced with her and he began to like her. However, her magic time ran out and Cinderella fled, leaving her glass slipper behind her.

KEY MOMENT 5: The prince wanted to find out who she was, so he took the glass slipper and called to every house asking each woman to try it on. Cinderella's family tried to hide her from the prince, but he found her, gave her the slipper and they lived happily ever after.

Sample questions

Question 1 and sample answers　　　　　**25 marks**

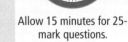

Read parts (c), (d), (e) and (f) below and then choose a
novel or a short story you have studied.

Allow 15 minutes for 25-mark questions.

(a) Name of novel or short story: *Of Mice and Men*

(b) Author: *John Steinbeck*

(c) If you could ask a character from your chosen text an interesting question
about something he or she did, what would the question be?

Name of character: *George Milton*

The interesting question I would ask is:
'How did you feel when you talked with Lennie, just before you shot him?'

(d) What answer do you think the character would give? You may answer as the
character.

*My heart was breakin' when I was talkin' to Lennie. I knew I had to act all
normal or he'd know there was something up. It was important to make sure
he felt safe and normal because he was my best friend. I wanted him to die
peacefully instead of being beaten up by the guys. He would've been scared
so I just kept focusing on that thought. It was the hardest conversation I
have ever had to have, and it was the hardest thing I've ever had to do.*

(e) Would you like to have this character as a friend? Give a reason for your answer.

[P] *I would like to have George as a friend because he cared about his friend.*

[I] *This is shown in the quote: 'Ever'body gonna be nice to you. Ain't gonna be
no more trouble.'*

[E] *This tells us that George is trying to make Lennie feel happy before his
death. He is a good friend because he doesn't want to be the one to kill his
friend, but he does it anyway, so Lennie won't feel any pain or suffering.
George will feel guilty for the rest of his life, but he is willing to go through
with it because he is a loyal friend.*

(f) If you could add a completely new character to the novel or short story you
have chosen, what would that character be like and what would he or she
do? Explain your answer.

[P] *If I could add a new character, it would be someone who would stop Lennie
killing Curley's wife.*

[I] *Both Lennie and Curley's wife end up dead because of Lennie's panic. If he
had another friend that looked out for him in the same way George did,
then maybe they both wouldn't have died.*

[E] *I felt very sad at the end of the story because I knew that Lennie didn't
mean to do it. Curley's wife was also a sad case and she could have gone on
to become a star or marry someone nicer than Curley.*

Question 2   25 marks

(a) Name your novel/short story:

_____

(b) Name the author:

_____

15

Allow 15 minutes for
25-mark questions.

Read parts (c), (d) and (e) below and then choose a novel or a short story you
have studied.

Pick one relationship and explain why it ended up working or breaking down
at the end of the story.

(c) One relationship I have studied is between ...

_____

_____

_____

_____

_____

_____

_____

(d) If your character was to give advice to another character, what would they tell
them?

I think the character _____ would tell ...

_____

_____

_____

_____

_____

(e) Imagine a different ending for your character. What would happen?

I imagine a different ending in which ... _____

_____

_____

_____

_____

_____

_____

Themes

A theme is the main topic or issue in a text. For each of your studied texts, you can have more than one theme to discuss. Look at the list of themes below and decide if any of them suit your studied novel.

- Love
- Hate
- Conflict
- Place
- Loneliness
- War

- Bullying
- Violence
- Childhood
- Mystery
- Religion
- Class

- Race
- Power
- Family
- Gender
- Poverty
- Suffering

When you are discussing your theme, it is important that you pick **at least two key moments** that show the theme in action. Pay particular attention to the opening and ending of the story.

When studying your novel, you should:

exam focus

> You should be able to write at least six or seven sentences about your key moment. Aim for more if you have the time in your exam.

1. Decide what the **main theme** of the novel is.
2. Make a list of **other themes** dealt with in the novel.
3. Examine the **opening of the novel**. How does it set up the theme?
4. Pick **three key moments** that show the main theme in action.
5. Examine the **ending of the novel**. What do you think the **overall message** is?

Phrases to help you discuss your theme:

I believe that the main theme is ...

There are lots of themes in this text, but the strongest one is ...

The theme of _____ is very important because ...

The author wants the reader to think of _____

The character has to deal with _____

The theme _____ is shown throughout the text ...

It is very interesting to explore the theme of _____

Read the following example based on *The Outsiders* by S.E. Hinton.

1. The main theme of *The Outsiders* is class conflict. This means that there are two different groups of people who belong to different classes: the rich and the poor.

2. Other themes are violence, friendship, loyalty and isolation.

3. The opening of the novel sets up the theme of class conflict. The protagonist and narrator is Ponyboy Curtis, and he tells us that he is a Greaser, a member of a gang who come from the East side of town. Greasers are poorer and wilder than their rivals, the Socs, who live on the West side of town. However, Socs are also violent and will jump on any Greaser walking by himself. Ponyboy tells us that he is living with his two brothers but that his parents have died. They have to struggle to live by themselves and keep themselves out of trouble. This shows us that Greasers don't have a lot of help from the State and that they struggle to survive.

4. One important moment in the novel is when Ponyboy gets jumped/beaten up by the Socs on his way home from the movies. This is important because it sets up more anger and tension between the Socs and the Greasers. Another key moment is when one of the Greasers tries to defend Ponyboy and stabs one of the Socs. This is important because they must now go on the run and hide from the Socs. Another key moment is when the Socs and the Greasers have a huge fight and, as a result, two of Ponyboy's friends die. This is important because it shows that all the conflict has led to the deaths of three people.

5. The ending of the novel shows the impact that the conflict has had on Ponyboy. He has to go to court to get permission to allow him stay with his two brothers. His grades are slipping even though he is an intelligent boy. It shows the effect that the violence, fear and deaths of three people have had on Ponyboy.

exam Q

Sample questions

Questions *25 marks*

Choose a novel or short story you have studied.

(a) Name of novel or short story: _____

(b) Name of author: _____

(c) Name the main theme of the story: _____

_____

(d) Describe a moment that you think deals with this theme:

_____

_____

_____

_____

_____

_____

_____

15

Allow 15 minutes for
25-mark questions.

(e) Did you enjoy this moment?

_____

_____

_____

_____

_____

_____

exam focus

Look back to page 27 for
words and phrases to help
you express your opinion.

(f) Do you think the theme was interesting? Give reasons for your answer.

_____

_____

_____

_____

_____

_____

_____

Picking your key moments

A **key moment** will have the following:
- It will involve one or more of the **main characters**
- It usually contains **drama or tension**
- It often **changes the course of the story** or has an **impact on** the main characters
- It often tells us about a **theme or relationship**

Sample question and answers

Questions   *20 marks*

Allow 12 minutes for 20-mark questions.

Choose a novel or short story you have studied.
(a) Name of novel or short story: *Lord of the Flies*

(b) Name of author: *William Golding*

(c) Describe a moment that you think was full of drama:

One key moment that is full of drama is when Piggy is killed with the giant boulder. The build-up to this moment is full of tension and drama because it is the last chance for Ralph and Piggy to try and convince the others that rules and order are important. In this key moment, Jack and Roger show that there is no turning back for them: they have become completely violent and savage. When they kill Piggy, they don't care about what they have done and go on to try and kill Ralph as well. Jack and the boys have lost any part of them that is human. We feel so sorry for Piggy, and we feel scared for Ralph because he could die too.

(d) If you could give one piece of advice to one of your main characters during this scene, what would it be?

[P] *If I could give one piece of advice, I would give it to Ralph.*

[I] *Ralph really believed that he could go down to the boys on the beach and demand Piggy's glasses back.*

[E] *My advice to him would be to be more careful about going down there at all. If he had waited or maybe picked a time where the boys were not so wild, they might have listened to him. My advice is that he needed to really think about how dangerous the boys had become and how much they didn't like himself and Piggy. If he had listened to my advice, maybe Piggy wouldn't have died.*

Time to practise

Sample questions

Questions   *20 marks*

Choose a novel or short story you have studied.

(a) Name_____

(b) Name of novel or short story: _____

(c) Name of author: _____

12

Allow 12 minutes for
20-mark questions.

(d) Describe a moment that you think was full of drama:

_____

_____

_____

_____

_____

_____

_____

_____

_____

(e) If you could give one piece of advice to one of your main characters during
this scene, what would it be?

_____

_____

_____

_____

_____

_____

_____

_____

_____

_____

_____

Comparing two novels or short stories

One thing you could be asked to do is to compare two novels or short stories, or a novel with a short story. What does it mean to compare?

Comparing
Means picking out things that are similar (the same) or different between the two stories.

Things to compare

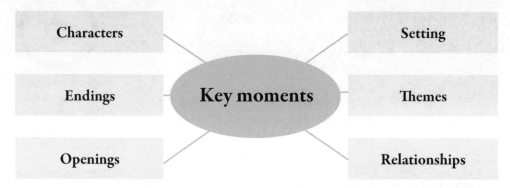

Characters

Setting

Endings

Key moments

Themes

Openings

Relationships

It is useful to use Venn diagrams when you are trying to work out your comparisons.

Example – *Little Red Riding Hood* and *The Three Little Pigs*

Little Red Riding Hood   *The Three Little Pigs*

Differences
The woodcutter saves the day

A mix of human and animal characters

Similar
Dangerous wolves

Wolves die

Violence

Family members

Differences
No humans – only animal characters

The pigs themselves save the day

There are particular words you need to use if you are comparing:

For **similarities** (saying something is the same):

- Similarly
- In the same way
- Both
- This is exactly like
- Just as

For **contrast** (saying something is different):

- In contrast
- Unlike
- This is different to
- However

How to use these phrases:

Little Red Riding Hood is **just like** *The Three Little Pigs* in that they **both** have mean wolves as the villain in their stories. In *Little Red Riding Hood*, the wolf is violent and wants to eat Little Red Riding Hood and her granny. **Similarly**, in *The Three Little Pigs*, the wolf is sneaky and wants to eat the three little pig brothers. **However, unlike** in *Little Red Riding Hood*, the pigs are able to save themselves, but Little Red Riding Hood and Granny are rescued by the woodcutter.

exam Q

Sample questions

Questions   *15 marks*

Compare your two novels or short stories or a novel and a short story.

(a) Name the novels/short stories:

_____

_____

_____

Allow 10 minutes for 15-mark questions.

(b) Name the authors:

_____

_____

(c) Finish the sentences below:

The main characters of my two stories are different because …

_____

_____

One similarity between my two stories is …

_____

_____

The setting of both stories is …

_____

_____

_____

The two stories are unlike each other because …

_____

_____

_____

_____

Cheat Sheet: Answering questions on your studied novels

You **must:**

1. **Spell** the name of your **novel** and its **author** correctly ◯
2. Identify **key moments** ◯
3. Describe **characters and relationships** ◯
4. Use **punctuation and grammar** correctly ◯
5. Discuss **themes and moments of change** ◯
6. Use **quotes** and **PIE** ◯
7. Learn words to **compare novels** ◯

You **should:**

8. Learn **key words** for your **characters** ◯
9. Know the character's **point of view** ◯
10. Learn about **the author** and **why the novel was written** ◯
11. Discuss the **way a novel is written** ◯

You **could:**

12. Use a variety of **interesting vocabulary** ◯

7 Drama

I will learn to:
- Understand acting techniques
- Understand how to use the stage
- Discuss stagecraft
- Describe key moments
- Identify themes

Drama – the basics

- Plays are first written as scripts and then they are given to directors and actors to bring those words to life.
- People who write plays are called playwrights.
- A playwright will write a script which gives the director and actors stage directions. These are really helpful when it comes to putting on (or staging) the play in a theatre.

Acting techniques and using the stage

When actors get their scripts, they must decide how they will perform the words on the page. They really think about their character and how they will act on stage.

Actors need to think about their character's emotions and what physical actions they can use on stage to show these emotions to the audience (for example, crying, laughing, fidgeting, sitting very still and not moving, being restless and unable to sit still and so on).

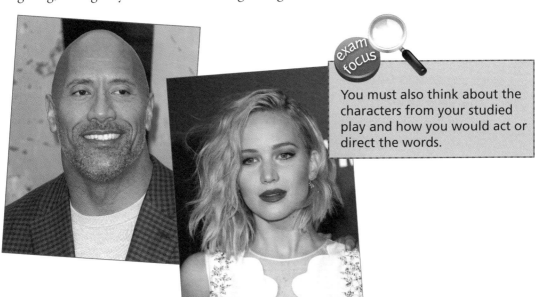

exam focus

You must also think about the characters from your studied play and how you would act or direct the words.

List of things to think about as an actor:

- What kind of personality does the character have?
- Do they have a physical disability?
- Do they have any personal habits or show unusual behaviours?
- How loud would they be in a conversation with other people?
- Would they move quickly or slowly around the room?
- Would they talk at a fast or a slow pace?
- Do they carry any props?
- Are they likeable or would an audience hate them?

Using the stage

Actors and directors use the stage in many different ways to try and tell a story.

It can be divided into different sections to show different rooms, times or places, for example, a bedroom and sitting room, or outside and inside a house.

Raised platforms or scaffolding can also be used to create a picture for the audience.

Actors need to be careful about where they move on the stage so that it makes sense to the audience.

Sample questions and answers

Questions   *25 marks*

Choose a play you have studied.

(a) Name the play: ___Romeo and Juliet___

(b) Name the playwright: ___William Shakespeare___

Allow 15 minutes for 25-mark questions.

(c) Imagine you are an actor and you are being interviewed about how you become a character from your studied play. Write the answers to the questions that follow:

Interviewer: Hello, thank you for this interview today. What is the name of your character?

Actor: Romeo from Romeo and Juliet.

Interviewer: What type of personality does your character have?

Actor: Romeo is very quick to fall in love with Juliet, so he is passionate. He can only think of Juliet and is obsessed with her. He doesn't really think about the consequences when he falls in love with someone from an enemy house, so he is a little thoughtless. Romeo is too much in love to notice the things around him.

Interviewer: When do things change for your character?

Actor: When Romeo kills Tybalt, things change for him because he is banished (not allowed live in the city any more). If he is caught, he will be killed. This means he can't be with his love, Juliet. These changes lead to his death and Juliet's death at the end of the play.

Interviewer: As an actor, how did you say your lines? What kind of voice did you use?

Actor: I said my lines with lots of energy because Romeo is young. Mostly, I talked quickly and my voice was loud.

Interviewer: Did you like playing your character?

Actor: I did like playing Romeo. He is full of energy and drama and there is never a boring moment with him. I don't think the decisions he makes are always good, but as an actor, this is good because I get to do lots of different things on stage.

exam Q

Sample questions

Questions   *25 marks*

Choose a play you have studied.

(a) Name the play: _____

(b) Name the playwright: _____

Allow 15 minutes for 25-mark questions.

(c) Imagine you are an actor and you are being interviewed about how you become a character from your studied play. Write the answers to the questions that follow:

Interviewer: Hello, thank you for this interview today. What is the name of your character?

Actor:

exam focus

_____

Interviewer: What type of personality does your character have?

Aim to write three or four sentences per answer.

Actor:

_____
_____
_____
_____
_____

Interviewer: When do things change for your character?

Actor:

_____

_____

_____

_____

_____

Interviewer: As an actor, how did you say your lines? What kind of voice did you use?

Actor:

_____

_____

_____

_____

_____

Interviewer: Did you like playing your character?

Actor:

_____

_____

_____

_____

_____

Understanding stagecraft

Stagecraft is what people use to bring a play to life. It involves using costume, lighting, set, scenery and backdrops, sound and props to help an audience believe they are part of the characters' world.

Costume

This is very important to the actors and the audience to bring a character to life. As soon as an actor puts on a costume, they will feel more like the character they are playing.

These are some things to think about when looking at a costume:

- What colour is it?
- What shape is it?
- What material is used?
- Does the character have more than one costume?

Let's look at an example:

The Wicked Witch, Elphaba, is a character from *The Wizard of Oz* and the musical, *Wicked*.

Her costume is black, but she has a green face and green hands.

- She wears a pointy hat that makes her look cruel and scary. She wears a long top and long skirt.
- The material in her clothes looks like cotton, which is nothing special.
- In the *Wizard of Oz*, the character doesn't change her costume for the whole story. In the musical, *Wicked*, the character changes from a student at school to the Wicked Witch of the West, so her costume changes too.

Lighting

Stage lighting helps create mood and atmosphere, as well as lighting the actors and the stage. Here are some things to think about when looking at lighting:

- Is there lighting to show daytime or night-time?
- Are there spotlights to highlight characters or particular parts of the stage?
- Are there any scenes that use flashing lighting (strobe lighting) to create drama?
- Does any of the lighting reflect the weather?

Let's look at an example:

The Tempest is a play written by William Shakespeare. Below is a scene from a production of that play.

- The lighting is bright and the background is multi-coloured, which makes the stage look magical and dream-like.
- The characters at the front and centre of the stage are lit up; we can see that they are happy and dancing, and they are wearing bright costumes.
- There are two onlookers on either side of the stage who are lit up by spotlights – this draws our attention to them and suggests that they might be important characters.

Set, scenery and backdrops

The stage set is usually made up of scenery and backdrops, which are painted or drawn with scenes or designs to suggest the place and time where the play is happening. Here are some things to think about when looking at the set and backdrops:

- Is the stage set realistic or does it just create an impression of a place or time?
- What is on the backdrop or scenery – is it simplistic or detailed?
- Is the set, backdrop or scenery fixed or movable?
- Does the set, backdrop or scenery change for different scenes?

Let's look at an example:

An Inspector Calls is a play written by J. B. Priestley. The play is set in the dining room of a very wealthy house in 1912. The characters start the play in the middle of a dinner party.

- The set has a fireplace with a framed picture above it. The scenery/backdrop walls on either side of the fireplace are covered with fancy wallpaper. There is a beautiful lamp and ornate clock on top of the fireplace.
- The backdrop or scenery is detailed and realistic – the set looks like a real 1912 room.
- The set doesn't change because they are in that room for the entire (whole) play.

Music and sound effects

Music and sounds are important to add atmosphere and help create the world of the play. Here are some things to think about when looking at sound:

- Is there any use of music?
- Are there any sound effects?

Let's look at an example:

The War Horse is adapted by Nick Stafford and based on a novel by Michael Morpurgo. This play features a puppet horse and the horse is one of the main characters of the play.

- There is music at times, but it is not a main feature of the play.
- There are sound effects for the noise of the horse. There are also sounds of war, like gunshots and explosions, because the play is set during World War I.

Props

Props (short for 'properties') are objects an actor uses during the play. Props can be realistic or symbolic (for example, a blue cloth to indicate water). Background props are props which may be part of the set, such as tables and chairs and so on. Here are some things to think about when looking at props:

- Does any character have a special prop that belongs to their character only?
- Are the props of the time or are they modern? For example, in modern productions of Shakespeare, guns are often used instead of swords.
- Are there any background props that are not used by the characters?

Let's look at an example:

Alone it Stands is a play by John Breen. It is about the 1978 rugby match between Munster and New Zealand where the Irish team beat the All Blacks.

- Characters don't use specific props, instead, the actors use their bodies to make the shape of a prop, for example, a car.
- The fact that the production doesn't use a lot of props is unusual, but it is also simple and effective.
- The play has no set, but some productions use background props, such as goalposts and hospitals beds.

Time to practise

Write down two sentences describing each feature of stagecraft based on your studied play.

Costume _____

_____

_____

_____

_____

Lighting _____

_____

_____

_____

_____

Music and sound effects _____

_____

_____

_____

_____

Set, scenery and backdrops _____

_____

_____

_____

_____

Props _____

_____

_____

_____

_____

Describing key moments

- Just like for your novel, you need to know at least **three key moments** in your studied play. However, a play is different to a novel because you may be asked to talk about **stagecraft**. You should be able to talk about **the opening, the ending** and **one other key moment** from the play.
- You may also be asked to describe the key moment and discuss the **relationships** going on between the **characters** in it.
- You could also be asked about the use of stagecraft in that key moment.
- When you discuss your key moment, you should be able to explain why it is an important moment in the story, but you should also be able to say why you think an audience might enjoy this scene.

Here are some phrases to help you discuss the last two points above:

This scene is important because …

This is an essential moment for the main character because …

An audience would enjoy this scene …

An audience would be shocked …

The scene is full of drama and tension …

It was great to see …

An audience might be uncomfortable during this scene …

The use of lighting/costume/props/set, scenery and backdrops/sound is very effective …

An audience would appreciate …

The character's costume helps me/the audience believe in the character and the story.

The lighting convinced me/the audience that I was/they were in the middle of a storm.

The sound effects added to the scary atmosphere.

The set, scenery and backdrops made the setting realistic; I believed I was there.

The props were really realistic and helped me believe in the character.

Vocabulary to help you discuss stagecraft:

Costume

Oversized **Hat** Dark

Cotton Old Tight **Detailed**

Attractive Fancy **Leather**

New Dress

Colourful Corset Plain

Boring Shabby **Long** *Silk*

Short Suit **Ugly** Shiny

Lighting

Dark	Mood lighting
Bright	Romantic
Daylight	Harsh
Night-time	Soft
Realistic	Flickering
Artificial (not natural)	

Set, Scenery and Backdrop

Detailed	Natural	
Simple	City	
Realistic	Countryside	
Stylised	Landscape	
Imaginative	Fixed	
Atmospheric	Changing	

Music and Sound Effects

Loud Beat
Fast Slow Catchy
Depressing Gentle Upbeat
Quiet Sharp Cheerful
Booming (loud)

Props

Personal (to a specific actor)

Modern (new/up-to-date)

Traditional (old)

Period (belonging to a particular historical time)

Realistic

Symbolic

Sample question and answer

Question   *15 marks*

1. Choose a key moment from a play you have studied and describe some of the things you would see on stage if you were sitting in the audience.
   You can talk about costume, set and backdrop, props and lighting

Allow 10 minutes for 15-mark questions.

(a) Name of play: *Blood Brothers*

(b) Name of playwright: *Willy Russell*

One of the key moments that is important to the play is when Eddie and Mickey meet each other for the first time. I think

costume ▷ *Mickey would be wearing very **old clothes** that are torn because he comes from a poor background. Eddie would be in a very **fancy** school uniform with long socks and a blazer. I also*

prop ▷ *think Eddie should carry a **bag of sweets** because Mickey asks him for one and that's how they talk to each other and become*

set backdrop ▷ *friends. The set backdrop is a **detailed drawing of council houses** because that's where Mickey is from.*

key point

The example on the previous page uses words and phrases from the lists on pages 93–94. When you are practising, try to use words and phrases from these lists to help you create your sentences and paragraphs.

exam Q

Sample questions

Questions   *15 marks*

Choose a play you have studied. Imagine you are directing that play and describe the costumes and props you would give to one character at a key moment in the story.

(10)

Allow 10 minutes for 15-mark questions.

(a) Name of play: _____

(b) Name of playwright: _____

(c) Name of character: _____

(d) Describe a key moment:

_____

_____

_____

_____

_____

(e) Describe the costume and why the character is wearing it:

_____

_____

_____

_____

_____

(f) Describe the props and why the character is using them:

_____

_____

_____

_____

_____

Identifying themes

Like for your novel, you should be able to identify one main theme for your play. You should also know about three other themes that come up throughout the story.

- Identify your main theme.
- Think about key moments that show the theme.
- Is the theme shown in a positive or negative way?
- How does the theme end up?

Sample questions

Question 1 and sample answers   **25 marks**

Imagine you are one of the characters from your studied play and you are writing an email to tell another character how you feel about them.

Allow 15 minutes for 25-mark questions.

(a) Name of play: *The Merchant of Venice*

(b) Name of character: *Bassanio*

To: Portia@belmontcaskets.ore

From: Bassanio@venice.it

Re: My love for you

Portia,

I write to you because I am madly in love with you. When I saw you, I fell in love with you at that very moment. You are beautiful, Portia, and I know I don't deserve you because I don't have any money, but I am trying to change that.

I plan to come to your house and pick a casket. I hope it will be the right one, so I can marry you. I plan to get a loan with the help of my friend, Antonio, so I can arrive in style and impress you. It is very difficult to get a loan, but I'm hoping that the local Jewish moneylender, Shylock, will give Antonio the loan to help me.

I don't know how you feel about me because we only met that once, but I hear you don't like your suitors, so I am hoping that there is a space in your heart for me. Please consider me for your husband. I will do my best to make you happy.

Lots of love,

Bassanio

Question 2   15 marks

Choose one play you have studied and identify the main
theme of the story. Finish the sentences below about
your chosen play:

10

Allow 10 minutes for
15-mark questions.

(a) Name of play: _____

(b) Theme: _____

(c) I think _____ is the main theme in the play because ...

_____

_____

_____

_____

(d) A key moment that really shows this theme is when ...

_____

_____

_____

_____

(e) I thought this theme was really interesting because ...

_____

_____

_____

_____

_____

_____

Sometimes you might be asked to study a photo or read part of a script. Practise answering these questions about drama productions:

Sample questions

Questions   *20 marks*

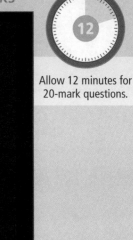

Allow 12 minutes for 20-mark questions.

Study the image above, which is from a production of *West Side Story* written by Arthur Laurents, with music by Leonard Bernstein and lyrics by Stephen Sondheim. This musical play is about two gangs from New York who fight over who gets to own the streets they all live on. The two gangs are called the Jets and the Sharks.

(a) This play is set on the streets of New York. What parts of the set and backdrop make it look like that?

_____

_____

(b) Describe the lighting in the picture.

_____

_____

(c) Describe the costumes the men are wearing.

_____

_____

(d) If you were to add one thing to the stage, what would it be and why?

_____

_____

Exam Question 2017 (Junior Cycle 2017, Final Examination, English, Ordinary Level)

Questions   *20 marks*

You have been given the job of directing a play that you studied.

(a) Name the play that you studied:

_____

Allow 12 minutes for 20-mark questions.

(b) Name an important character from your chosen play:

_____

(c) Describe a key moment in the play where your named character plays a significant role:

_____

_____

_____

_____

_____

_____

_____

_____

_____

_____

_____

(d) Did you like or dislike what your named character did in the key moment you have described? Give a reason for your answer.

_____

_____

_____

_____

_____

_____

_____

_____

Cheat Sheet: Answering questions on drama and your studied plays

You **must**:

1. Know your **main characters** ◯
2. Be able to **describe what happens** in at least **three** key moments ◯
3. Be able to **talk about acting** ◯
4. Be able to describe how a **scene would look on a stage** ◯
5. Identify **themes** ◯
6. Answer on your **studied play** (not the film) ◯
7. Use correct **punctuation and grammar** ◯
8. Use **PIE** when answering ◯
9. Learn the **correct spelling** of the name of the **play** and **playwright** ◯

You **should**:

10. Learn **key vocabulary and phrases** to help you ◯
11. Understand the main character's **point of view** ◯
12. Give **your own opinion** about the play or character ◯

You **could**:

13. Use a **variety of different vocabulary** when answering questions ◯

8 Film

Film – the basics

- Film is a story or event that is filmed on camera. It is shown in cinemas or can be watched at home.
- Directors are the people who direct the film and have the final say about everything.
- There are many people who work on a film to make it into a story, including actors, camera and sound technicians, film editors and many more.
- Filmmakers have the time and technology to make their story look and sound as realistic and true to life as they want.

There are many different genres and types of film:

Romcom	a romantic comedy
Sci-fi	science fiction, which can feature space, time travel or aliens
Thriller	features a storyline full of tension and suspense
Action/adventure	features a storyline where the main character (protagonist) experiences threat or danger and exciting chases
Horror	features a story that scares the audience
Animation	is made up of drawings or paintings, puppets or models which move on screen
Documentary	features real-life footage (recordings)
Western	features cowboys
Crime	involves detectives and investigators who solve crimes and catch criminals
War	features stories about what happens during a war
Fantasy	features stories with magic or magical creatures and supernatural events

Answering questions on film

Look at this example:

Sometimes, you are given the option to answer a question on your studied film. This means that you need to know your studied film's plot (storyline), characters and key moments very well.

Sample questions and answers

Question 1   *20 marks*

You have been given the job of directing a film that you studied.

(a) Name the film that you studied: *Bend It Like Beckham*

(b) Name an important character from your chosen film: *Jess*

(c) Describe a key moment in the film where your named character plays a significant role.

Allow 12 minutes for 20-mark questions.

A key moment that I have studied is when Jess finally tells her parents that she wants to play football. Jess is British, but her parents are from India. This means her parents and family have certain ideas about what she can do as a woman, and football is not one of them. Jess plays a significant role in this scene because she stands up for what she wants. In the key scene, all her family are listening to her in the sitting room as she tells them how she feels. She plays a significant role by being brave and telling the truth, even though it is hard for her and her parents.

(d) Did you like or dislike what your named character did in the key moment you have described? Give a reason for your answer.

I really liked what Jess did in this scene because it showed that she was brave and knew what she wanted. All along, she was trying to please her parents but, in this scene, she decided to stand up for herself, and this is something that I admired.

(e) Give one piece of advice to an actor playing the part of your named character, about how he or she should act during this key moment. Why do you think this piece of advice would help the actor to play the part well?

The one of piece of advice that I would give to this actor is not to cry. Even though she is upset, Jess is not the type of girl who would easily cry. She would be angry and fight her case, but she wouldn't allow herself to get too upset in front of her family.

Question 2

In this next question you are asked to say why your chosen character is interesting. Examine some of the possible reasons to see if they apply to the main characters in your film:

key words

Brave	Overcomes a problem	Friendly
Rebellious	Cheeky	Mature
Kind	Strong	Lovable
Caring	Pitiful	Cheerful
Funny	Romantic	Dramatic
Role model	Wise	
Intelligent	Loyal	

When you have decided how you feel about your character – for example:

[P] *I feel my character is interesting because they are funny*
Be able to give an example to back up your point.

(a) Name the film that you studied:
Son of Rambow

(b) Name an important character from your chosen film: *Will Proudfoot*

[P] *I feel my chosen character, Will Proudfoot, is interesting because he is rebellious.*

[I] *Will sneaks out of his house to go and make a film with Lee Carter even though it is against his family's religion.*

Now you must keep answering the question but also give your own opinion.

[E] *I think Will is really rebellious because his family's religion is very strict, but he just wants to be a film star. He knows he will get in trouble, and his mam will be disappointed if he is caught, but he does it anyway.*

How to describe a scene

Here are some useful words and phrases that will help you describe a scene:

The scene I am going to discuss is …

In the opening/middle/end of the film …

The main characters involved are …

This scene is important/interesting/a key moment because …

An audience would enjoy/dislike this scene because …

This moment makes you/me feel like …

The action in this scene is very exciting and thrilling …

This scene makes you feel really uncomfortable because …

In this scene, the character shows their true personality …

This scene affects the rest of the story …

This scene was really …

When you are discussing a key moment in a film, you should use some film language.

- Dramatic
- Sad
- Uplifting
- Exciting
- Powerful
- Comical (funny)
- Inspiring
- Tense (full of tension)
- Thought-provoking
- Violent
- Disappointing

key words

- **Scene** – a sequence of shots or actions
- **Costume** – the clothes an actor wears to help them become the character they are playing
- **Music** – sound and music are used in a film to accompany the action and create atmosphere
- **Lighting** – used to light the actors and the scene in a realistic or atmospheric way

Costume

Costume is really important to help an audience believe in a character. Costume refers to any clothes worn by a character in the film. Actors also use make-up and wigs to help people believe in their character.

Some examples of costume are:

- Hats
- Glasses
- Dresses
- Trousers

- Tops
- Shirts/blouses
- Jackets
- Scarves

- Underwear
- Shoes
- Bags

Some words to describe costumes:

- Realistic
- Fancy
- Worn
- Ragged
- Stylish

- Boring
- Smart
- Casual
- Fashionable
- Elegant

- Baggy
- Tight
- Old-fashioned
- Oversized
- Small

exam Q

Sample questions and answers

Questions   15 marks

(a) Name the film that you studied: *Sing Street*

(b) Name an important character from your chosen film: *Conor*

(c) Pick a key scene from your studied film and describe your character's costume.

Allow 10 minutes for 15-mark questions.

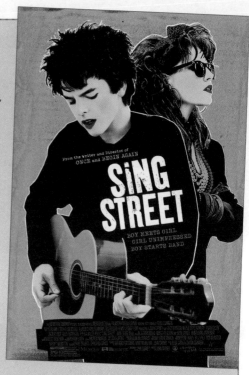

[P] *A key scene that I have studied is when Conor makes his first music video with the band and Raphina.*

[I] *He wears an oversized dark purple coat, a baggy shirt with a big floppy bow, green trousers and make-up.*

[E] *Before this scene, Conor looks like a normal teenage boy, but when he makes the video he dresses differently. This is unusual for Conor because he always wears normal clothes. This scene is important because it is the first time that they look like a serious band.*

(d) Explain why the costume is important to the character.

[P] *It is the first time Raphina sees Conor as a fun person because of his costume. This is important for their relationship.*

[I] *Raphina helps Conor put the costume together and she does his make-up.*

[E] *This is important because Raphina begins to care about Conor and the band. Conor's costume and makeover bring the two characters together to form a friendship. This then becomes a romance later on in the film.*

Music

Music and sound are really important to a film because they help create an atmosphere for the audience. If you watch a horror film, you will often hear a certain type of music that will make you feel uncomfortable. If you watch a romantic comedy, you will often hear music that will make you feel happy. If you watch an action/adventure film, you will often hear music that will make you feel excited or tense about what is going to happen.

Films can use popular songs, or they can use music that has been written specifically for them. If a film uses popular songs, it means that the audience will recognise them and this adds to the mood and atmosphere of a story. If a film uses original songs or music, this is called a score.

The following are different types of music that you might find in films:

- Instrumental
- Classical
- Opera
- Rock
- Pop
- Rap
- Country
- Hip-hop
- Electronic and bass
- Traditional

Here is some vocabulary to help you discuss music in your studied film:

- Instrumental
- Slow
- Fast
- Natural
- Soft

- Loud
- Shrill (high-pitched)
- Harsh
- Gentle
- Edgy (tense)

Sample questions and answers

Questions   *15 marks*

(a) Name the film that you studied: *Man on Wire*

(b) Pick a key scene from your studied film and describe how music helps to create the atmosphere of the scene.

Allow 10 minutes for 15-mark questions.

A key scene I have studied is Philippe Petit's tightrope walk across the Twin Towers in New York. The scene has photos of Petit's walk, along with interviews with different people. The music is slow, soft classical music. This helps create the atmosphere of wonder. People stop in the street to look up and wonder about what is happening above them. They are amazed at what they see. The music reflects the feelings of the people watching.

Usually, you would expect some tense music, but, instead, the scene uses classical music to make us really think about Petit's skill. The music plays alongside photos of Petit almost dancing along the thin wire. This makes us think of a ballet. The music helps us imagine that Petit is just a ballet dancer on a stage, not a tightrope walker walking between two buildings.

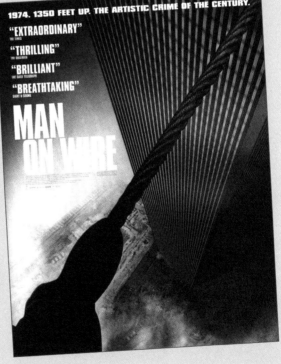

Lighting

Films also use lighting to create atmosphere, mood and meaning in a scene.

Here are some key words to help you discuss lighting:

- Natural
- Bright
- Dark
- Spotlight

- Shadow
- Low light
- Soft light
- Harsh light

Sample questions and answers

Question 1   15 marks

Allow 10 minutes for 15-mark questions.

(a) Name the film that you studied: *E.T. the Extra-Terrestrial*

(b) Pick a key scene from your studied film and explain what happens.

The scene I am going to discuss is when Elliott cuts his finger on a large saw razor. It hurts him, so he says, 'Ouch!' E.T. hears the word and repeats it. Then he uses the magical power in his own finger to make Elliott better. After Elliott's finger is healed, they both listen to Elliott's mother reading a bedtime story to his sister. She is reading Peter Pan and Tinkerbell is talking about believing in magic. Elliott looks at E.T. because he has just used his magic on him.

(c) Explain how this scene uses light to create an atmosphere or meaning.

This scene uses dark light and bright light to create meaning. At the beginning of the scene, E.T. is hiding in Elliott's big wardrobe. You can see the dark shadow of Elliott's mam against the white doors of the wardrobe. When Elliott comes in, he closes all the doors and blinds to make it even darker because he is trying to hide E.T. from his mam. When Elliott takes out the large saw razor, the light shines on it, making it look dangerous. He cuts his finger, but then E.T.'s finger lights up like the sun. The light

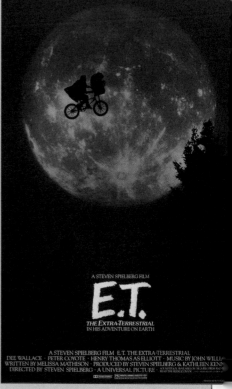

A STEVEN SPIELBERG FILM

E.T.

THE EXTRA-TERRESTRIAL
IN HIS ADVENTURE ON EARTH

A STEVEN SPIELBERG FILM E.T. THE EXTRA-TERRESTRIAL
DEE WALLACE · PETER COYOTE · HENRY THOMAS AS ELLIOTT · MUSIC BY JOHN WILLI·
WRITTEN BY MELISSA MATHISON · PRODUCED BY STEVEN SPIELBERG & KATHLEEN KENN·
DIRECTED BY STEVEN SPIELBERG · A UNIVERSAL PICTURE ·

travels across the room and Elliott's face, touching Elliott's finger to cure it. E.T.'s finger is bright like the sun because like the sun, E.T. gives life to things.

Question 2   25 marks

Choose a film that you have studied.

(a) Title of film: *Hotel Rwanda*

(b) Name of film director: *Terry George*

(c) Imagine you are a film reviewer on a television programme for young people. Write the script for a review of your chosen film using the questions below.

Allow 15 minutes for 25-mark questions.

Introduce the film.
The film I am reviewing is called Hotel Rwanda, and it is set in Africa in 1994. This film was nominated for many awards, including the Oscars.

Explain what the film was about.
It is about a man called Paul Rusesabagina who takes over a hotel and runs it with his family. In the film there are two groups of people: the Hutu and the Tutsi. The Hutu don't like the Tutsi because they have lighter skin, so they go on a killing spree against the Tutsi people. Almost 800,000 Tutsis are murdered in 100 days. Paul realises he must do something to help and uses the hotel to help keep refugees safe.

Talk about the most interesting character in the film.
Paul is a very interesting character because he risks his life to try and save as many people as he can. Soon he has hundreds of refugees in his hotel. He calls the people he knows and bribes other people to stop Hutu soldiers from attacking the hotel. He also convinces the Hutu general that the Americans are watching them. It shows that he is caring, clever and brave to do these things. He leaves his family to stay and save more people. In the end, his courage saves a lot of lives.

What did you like or dislike about the film?
I really liked Paul's character in this film because he stood up for what he believed in. I also like the way it focused on his story to tell us about the Rwandan genocide because if it just focused on all of the deaths, then it would be too sad to watch. I didn't really like the music because it wasn't very memorable. This is a very emotional film and it should have had better music.

How would you rate the film?
I would rate the film nine out of ten because I felt that the story was so interesting, and it was told very well. I was gripped by each scene, especially when the danger began. I would recommend it to anyone who likes history or likes to see how something good can happen in the middle of something terrible.

exam focus

Learn the vocabulary in this chapter and use it in your answers.

Cheat Sheet: Answering questions on your studied films

You **must**:

1. **Name** and be able to **spell** the **film title** and **director** ◯
2. Be able to **describe** what happens during **key scenes** ◯
3. Name the **main characters** ◯
4. Be able **to talk about** the main characters ◯
5. Be able to say why you **liked or disliked** the film ◯
6. Use **capital letters** and **spell** everything **correctly** ◯

You **should**:

7. Be able to discuss **lighting, costume and music** ◯
8. Use **PIE** ◯

You **could**:

9. **Research extra information** about the film ◯
10. Use **interesting vocabulary** ◯

9 Preparing for Poetry

Over the course of Junior Cycle English, you will read and understand a wide range of poetry. For your final exam you may be asked to examine an unseen poem. You may also be asked to write about a poem you have studied during your course. Below are some words associated with poetry. In the boxes below them are examples of different styles of poem.

Rhythm

Metaphor Rhyme

Simile

Repetition Exaggeration (Hyperbole)

Alliteration

I – RHYMING

JABBERWOCKY

'Twas brillig, and the slithy toves

Did gyre and gimble in the wade;

All mimsy were the borogoves,

And the mome raths outgrabe.

'Beware the Jabberwock, my son!

The jaws that bite, the claws that catch!

Beware the Jubjub bird, and shun

The frumious Bandersnatch!

By Lewis Carroll

II – STANZAS

I WANDERED LONELY AS A CLOUD

I

I wandered lonely as a cloud
That floats on high o'er vales and hills,
When all at once I saw a crowd,
A host, of golden daffodils;
Beside the lake, beneath the trees,
Fluttering and dancing in the breeze.

II

Continuous as the stars that shine
And twinkle on the milky way,
They stretched in never-ending line
Along the margin of a bay:
Ten thousand saw I at a glance,
Tossing their heads in sprightly dance.

By William Wordsworth

III – FREE VERSE AND REPETITION

Friends hurt and blame.

I hurt and blame.

Data limit exceeded.

Did they just say that?

I hurt.

I hurt.

I hurt.

Reading a poem for meaning

People experience poetry in different ways. However, if you keep these three questions in mind, they will help you understand any poem you read:

- What is the poet saying?
- How is the poet saying it?
- How do I feel about the poem?

Let's apply these questions to a simple poem:

Roses are Red

Roses are red,
Violets are blue.
Carnations are sweet,
And so are you.

And so are they
That send you this.
And when we meet,
We'll have a kiss.

What is the poet saying? The poet is saying how sweet the person they are writing to is. They are also showing their romantic interest in this person.

How is the poet saying it? They have compared the person to a carnation to show how sweet they are. The first verse (stanza) is all about the person the poet likes, and the second verse says that the poet is sweet too and wants a kiss.

How do I feel about the poem? I don't really like the poem. It's a bit silly and old-fashioned.

Unseen poetry

Poem 1 – Show my understanding of an unseen poem

If poetry is included in your exam, you will be given an unseen poem to look at. This is a poem that you have never seen before. You will be asked to read it and answer questions on it.

Remember the three questions above to help you understand the poem you are given.

> **What is the poet saying?**
> **How is the poet saying it?**
> **How do I feel about the poem?**

When answering questions on an unseen poem you must:

- Show a good understanding of the poem
- Give your opinion on the poem.

The New Kid on the Block

There's a new kid on the block,
and boy, that kid is tough,
that new kid punches hard,
that new kid plays real rough,
that new kid's big and strong,
with muscles everywhere,
that new kid tweaked my arm,
that new kid pulled my hair.

That new kid likes to fight,
and picks on all the guys,
that new kid scares me some,
(that new kid's twice my size),
that new kid stomped my toes,
that new kid swiped my ball,
that new kid's really bad,
I don't care for her at all.

by Jack Prelutsky

Sample questions and answers

Question 1   **5 marks**

Allow 3 minutes for 5-mark questions.

1. From your reading of the poem, write down the correct letter in the box provided.

   (a) The new kid is:

   A. Thin and weak

   B. Tall and awkward

   C. Big and strong   ✔

   D. Small and round

(b) The new kid has:
   A. Stones in their pockets ☐
   B. Food down their trousers ☐
   C. A rich uncle ☐
   D. Muscles everywhere ✔

(c) The speaker in the poem feels:
   A. Sad ☐
   B. Angry ☐
   C. Scared ✔
   D. Happy ☐

(d) This poem has:
   A. Two stanzas ✔
   B. Three stanzas ☐
   C. Six stanzas ☐
   D. No stanzas ☐

(e) The new kid:
   A. Took the speaker's ball ✔
   B. Stole the speaker's schoolbag ☐
   C. Wrote a nasty note ☐
   D. Played a trick on a teacher ☐

Question 2   5 marks

2. If you were the speaker in the poem, what would worry you the most about the new kid?

Sample answer using PIE

[P] *I would be worried about the fact that the new kid punches and hits people.*

[I] *The speaker says the new kid 'punches hard', 'likes to fight' and 'stomped my toes'.*

[E] *Some of the bullying I can deal with, but I really don't like being hit.*

Time to practise

Poem 2 – Unseen poem

Read the following poem carefully and answer the questions that follow:

Lion

Poor prisoner in a cage,
I understand your rage
And why you loudly roar
Walking that stony floor.

Your forest eyes are sad
As wearily you pad
A few yards up and down,
A king without a crown.

Up and down all day,
A wild beast for display,
Or lying in the heat
With sawdust, smells and meat,

Remembering how you chased
Your jungle prey, and raced,
Leaping upon their backs
Along the grassy tracks.

But you are here instead,
Better, perhaps, be dead
Than locked in this dark den;
Forgive us, lion, then,
Who did not ever choose,
Our circuses and zoos.

by Leonard Clark

Sample questions

Question 1   *5 marks*
Write down two phrases the poet uses to describe the lion.

_____

_____

Question 2   *5 marks*

According to the poet, what does the lion probably think about each day?

_____

_____

_____

Question 3   *5 marks*

How do you think the poet feels about zoos and circuses?

_____

_____

_____

_____

Poem 3 – Give a personal response to a poem

The Beautiful Sky

Oh! It's such a beautiful blue sky!
Where the birds enjoy
And they merrily fly.

Oh! It's such a beautiful blue sky!
Where the clouds make their hive
And a joyful experience
To sit and spy.

Oh! It's such a beautiful blue sky!
A gorgeous place for the stars
To appear in the night
And spread out the light.

Oh! It's such a beautiful blue sky!
Oh! It's such a beautiful blue sky!
            by Deepanjali M. Kajagar

When responding to questions like the ones below, you must use the PIE format. This is explained on page 27.

Sample questions and answers

Question 1   10 marks

Did you like/dislike this poem? Give reasons for your answer.

Allow 6 minutes for 10-mark questions.

Sample answer using PIE

[P] *I really liked the poem 'The Beautiful Sky' by Deepanjali M. Kajagar.*

[I] *I think the poet creates some lovely images and gives a really positive message.*

[E] *The two images I liked best are 'the clouds make their hive' and 'a beautiful blue sky' because I can easily imagine these images. They are also really positive, and with words like 'beautiful', 'blue', 'gorgeous' and 'light', the message is that we should enjoy nature's good bits.*

Question 2   10 marks

Do you think the poet is in a happy or sad mood in this poem? Give reasons for your answer.

Sample answer using PIE

[P] *I think the poet is definitely in a happy mood in this poem.*

[I] *It's almost like they cannot say the sky is beautiful enough times and they only focus on the positive things about it.*

[E] *The line 'Oh! It's such a beautiful blue sky' is repeated five times in the poem, and the poet also uses exclamation marks to emphasise their point. They don't focus on rain or wind but the 'merry birds' and the 'bright stars'.*

Poem 4 – Personal response

Winter Days

Biting air
Winds blow
City streets
Under snow

Noses red
Lips sore
Runny eyes
Hands raw

Chimneys smoke
Cars crawl
Piled snow
On garden wall

Slush in gutters
Ice in lanes
Frosty patterns
On window panes

Morning call
Lift up head
Nipped by winter
Stay in bed

by Gareth Owen

Sample questions

Question 1   10 marks

Do you think this poem gives a positive or negative image of
winter time? Give reasons for your answer.

Allow 6 minutes for
10-mark questions.

_____

_____

_____

_____

Question 2   *10 marks*

Which line(s) do you think best represent **your** idea of winter? Give reasons for your answer.

_____

_____

_____

_____

_____

Question 3   *10 marks*

What do you think the poet means by the last stanza of the poem? Give reasons for your answer.

_____

_____

_____

_____

_____

Studied poetry

Revising different elements (parts) of poetry

key words

Speaker	Simile	Shape
Theme	Metaphor	Exaggeration
Message	Rhyme	Repetition
Alliteration	Verse	Image
Style	Rhythm	Tone/mood

What to look for when you're studying a poem:

Who is the speaker of the poem? The poet can be the speaker or sometimes the poet imagines someone else speaking.

What is the theme of the poem? Every poem is about something. Many themes are universal, for example, themes that everyone knows, like war, love and bullying.

What is the message of the poem? Poems usually have a message. For example, the poem 'Base Details' by Siegfried Sassoon has the theme of war, but the message is how pointless war is.

What is the tone or mood of the poem? Usually when you read a poem you get a sense of the mood or tone of the poem or how the poet is feeling. For example, the poem 'Mid-Term Break' by Seamus Heaney has a very sad tone because it is about the death of his younger brother.

What images does the poet create? Images are the pictures created in your mind when you read a selection of words or lines. In the poem 'The Mewlips', J.R.R. Tolkien creates creepy images of the disgusting Mewlip's home:

You should be familiar with what makes your studied poem stand out. Is it theme, structure, clever alliteration or onomatopoeia, or something else?

> Beside the rotting river-strand
> The drooping willows weep,
> And gloomily the gorcrows stand
> Croaking in their sleep.

What language devices does the poet use? Poets play with language and use different techniques to bring their images to life, such as repetition, alliteration, simile and descriptive adjectives and verbs. You will see more of these explained after the next poem.

What is the style or shape of the poem? Poems come in all shapes and sizes. Usually the poet has a good reason for structuring their poem in a certain way. Some poems have verses (stanzas) of equal length that rhyme, and other poets write in free verse where they don't follow any particular structure. For example, the poem 'Funeral Blues' by W.H. Auden has four stanzas of four lines each. Lines one and two and lines three and four rhyme in every verse. However, the poem 'Postscript' by Seamus Heaney is free verse.

The poems mentioned above are popular studied poems, and you may have studied some of them in English class. They can all be easily found online.

Poem 5 – Studied poetry

- To revise different elements (parts) of poetry
- To make a well-supported point about a poem you have read.

The things you learn about in your studied poetry can be applied to the unseen poetry on the exam paper.

Mid-Term Break

I sat all morning in the college sick bay,
Counting bells knelling classes to a close.
At two o'clock our neighbours drove me home.

In the porch I met my father crying –
He had always taken funerals in his stride –
And Big Jim Evans saying it was a hard blow.

The baby cooed and laughed and rocked the pram
When I came in, and I was embarrassed
By old men standing up to shake my hand

And tell me they were 'sorry for my trouble'.
Whispers informed strangers I was the eldest,
Away at school, as my mother held my hand

In hers and coughed out angry tearless sighs.
At ten o'clock the ambulance arrived
With the corpse, stanched and bandaged by the nurses.

Next morning I went up into the room. Snowdrops
And candles soothed the bedside; I saw him
For the first time in six weeks. Paler now,

Wearing a poppy bruise on his left temple,
He lay in the four foot box as in his cot.
No gaudy scars, the bumper knocked him clear.

A four foot box, a foot for every year.

by Seamus Heaney

Now apply the study questions that you learned on pages 119–20:

Who is the speaker of the poem? The poet is the speaker. He is talking about a childhood memory.

What is the theme of the poem? This poem's theme is personal loss or death.

What is the message of the poem? The message of the poem is that this was a difficult time in the speaker's childhood, and he will always remember it. The reader also sees that death is difficult for people.

What is the tone or mood of the poem? The tone/mood of the poem is sad as the speaker is describing a funeral scene for his little brother in his family home.

What images does the poet create?

- Waiting in the college sick bay
- Father in the porch
- Big Jim Evans
- His mother coughing out 'angry tearless sighs'
- The corpse
- Snowdrops and candles
- Four foot box
- Poppy bruise on little boy's head
- Coffin = cot

What language devices does the poet use?

- *Expressive adjectives and verbs* – Adjectives and verbs carefully chosen to give us a really clear image:
  - Angry, tearless, poppy, gaudy
  - Knelling, cooed, stanched, bandaged, soothed.
- *Simile* – Where a comparison is made using the words 'like' or 'as'.
  - 'the four foot box as in his cot.'
- *Direct speech* – Where the poet inserts exactly what a character says. It makes the scene more realistic.
  - 'sorry for my trouble'.
- *Onomatopoeia* – Where the word used sounds like the action: 'bells knelling', 'baby cooed', 'coughed'.
- *Personification* – Where the poet gives a non-human object human qualities or features. 'Snowdrops and candles soothed the bedside.' 'Soothe' is an action we expect from humans when they comfort someone but here Heaney has suggested that the candles and snowdrops are doing the action instead.

What is the style or shape of the poem?

This poem consists of seven stanzas (verses) of three lines each and one single line at the end. This brings nice even pace to the poem. Each stanza seems to be a new step on the speaker's journey. The single line at the end is separate to emphasise the tragedy of the poem. A four-year-old child has been knocked down and killed.

Other important language devices used by poets:

Rhyme – Where the sound of two or more words agree (have the same last sound), for example, 'table' and 'stable'.

Rhythm – The regular repeated beat/pattern of movement or sound.

Metaphors – Comparing things without using the words 'like', 'as' or 'than'. For example, if you say someone 'is a star', you don't mean they are an *actual* star, you just want to highlight that they have a shining talent or a bright future.

Repetition – Where the poet repeats certain words to emphasise their importance or the image they have created. '—until everything was rainbow, rainbow, rainbow!' (A line from Elizabeth Bishop's poem, 'The Fish'.)

Exaggeration (Hyperbole) – Where a poet exaggerates something to give it more impact: 'Well the playground was three miles long and the playground was five miles wide' (A line from Adrian Mitchell's poem 'Back in the Playground Blues'.)

Alliteration – This is where words beside or close to each other begin with the same sound. It adds rhythm and music to the poem. 'The woods are lovely, *d*ark and *d*eep,' (a line from Robert Frost's poem 'Stopping by Woods on a Snowy Evening').

If you are asked to write about a studied poem, you cannot use the poem printed on the exam paper.

Sample questions

Question 1 and sample answers   *20 marks*

Choose a poem you have studied where the poet deals with a theme that you found interesting or appealing. You may not use a poem printed on this paper.

Allow 12 minutes for 20-mark questions.

(a) Title of poem: 'The Lake Isle of Innisfree'

(b) Name of poet: W. B. Yeats

(c) What is the theme of your chosen poem? In what ways did you find it interesting or appealing?

[P] *The theme in 'The Lake Isle of Innisfree' that I found interesting was nature.*

[I] *The whole poem is about the speaker getting away to the lake isle of Innisfree. He makes it sound really appealing.*

[E] *The poet wants to build a cabin by the lake and have a 'hive for the honey bee'. He says that he will have 'some peace there'. The only things he will hear are the crickets and the linnets. I don't like being on my own, but he makes the island sound really nice with 'water lapping' and the sound of bees.*

(d) Would you recommend this poem to a friend? Give reasons for your answer.

[P] *I would definitely recommend this poem to a friend.*

[I] *The best part about the poem is that W. B. Yeats creates lovely images for the reader.*

[E] *I can imagine the cabin made from wattle and clay, and I love the image of the 'water lapping' on the shore.*

[I] *The second reason I would recommend it is that it makes me want to visit the lake isle of Innisfree.*

[E] *The poet really wants to go there, and he makes it sound really appealing. He sounds like he really misses life in the country when he says, 'on the pavements grey'.*

Question 2   20 marks

Choose a poem you have studied that had an interesting message.

Name of poem: _____

Name of poet: _____

Allow 12 minutes for 20-mark questions.

What was the message of the poem?

_____

_____

_____

_____

Why did you find it interesting?

_____

_____

_____

_____

Would you recommend this poem to a friend? Give reasons for your answer.

_____

_____

_____

_____

_____

_____

Cheat Sheet: Answering questions on studied and unseen poems

You **must**:

1. **Spell** the **name** of your studied poem and its **author correctly** ◯
2. Identify **poetic devices** that make the poem enjoyable ◯
3. Use **punctuation and grammar correctly** in your responses ◯
4. Discuss **themes** ◯
5. **Support your opinions** with evidence (**PIE structure**) ◯

You **should**:

6. Learn some **memorable quotes** from your studied poems ◯
7. Understand the **poet's reasons for writing** the poem ◯

You **could**:

8. Use a **variety of interesting vocabulary** when answering ◯

10 Language and Grammar

Capitals and full stops

Capitals

key point

Capital letters are used to show:

- The start of a sentence
- Names of people, places and brands
- The pronoun 'I'
- Books and film titles
- Days of the week and months of the year

Example 1:

Tom worked in the factory on Fleet Street for three years. He started in December 2012.

- 'Tom' gets a capital letter because it is someone's name and because it is the start of the sentence.
- 'Fleet Street' gets two capitals because it is the name of a place.
- 'December' gets a capital letter because it is the name of a month.

Example 2:

Queen Victoria was queen of England for 63 years, seven months and two days. She enjoyed writing letters and reading books. It is said that one of her favourite books was *Merkland*, a Scotch novel by Mrs Oliphant.

- 'Queen' in Queen Victoria gets a capital because it is a title or name.
- But 'queen' in queen of England does not receive a capital because it is not a specific name or title.
- 'England' receives a capital because it is the name of a country.
- 'It' gets a capital because it is the beginning of a sentence.
- '*Merkland*' gets a capital because it is the title of a novel.
- 'Scotch' gets a capital because it means from Scotland.
- 'Mrs Oliphant' receives capitals because it is the author's name.

Example 3:

> Several girls caused trouble in the class on Monday. The teacher was really disappointed with Claire, Mary and Jessica's behaviour. It was really annoying because it wasted a lot of class time.

- 'Several' and 'The' get capitals because they start sentences.
- 'Monday' gets a capital because it is the name of a day of the week.
- 'Claire', 'Mary' and 'Jessica' get capitals because they are people's names.
- 'It' must get a capital letter because it starts the sentence.

Time to practise

Correct the following paragraph by including capitals in the correct places.

> david knew he had to get his speech written for the school assembly. his school, mercy college, was welcoming president higgins. david was going to say a few words on behalf of his fellow students. his best friend, sarah, had helped him write most of it, but now he was really nervous and didn't want to make a fool of himself in front of the president.

Full stops

Example 1:

> Aoife started playing football when she was four. She loved it straight away, and when she turned six, her mum took her to the local training camp. Aged seven, she was the best player on the under-8 team. It was really disappointing when she had to move to a different team. Her local club didn't have a girls' team, and she wasn't allowed to play with the boys any more when she turned 11.

key point

Full stops are used
- To end a sentence
- To give dramatic effect
- After initials
- For abbreviations (shortening a word or phrase)
- In price numbers

- The full stops are used above to show where a sentence ends.

Example 2:

'What did you think of the match, Sean?'

'Greatest. Game. Ever. From the time it started at 5:30p.m., it was exciting and entertaining.'

'How much was your ticket?'

'€19.99.'

- Full stops are used above to give dramatic effect to Sean's answer: 'Greatest. Game. Ever.'
- A full stop is used before and after 'p' and 'm' in p.m. because the letters are short for *post meridiem* (after midday).
- A full stop is used to end the sentence.
- A full stop is used to separate the numbers in the price of the ticket.

Time to practise

Correct the following piece by inserting capital letters and full stops.

jeff was the eldest son of abbie and tim wilson he was top of his class in all his subjects his English teacher, mr taylor, said he could become the new stephen king jeff didn't like the idea of becoming a writer he wanted to become a professional athlete

Commas

Example 1

My favourite flowers are roses, lilies, peonies and sunflowers. If I had to choose one, it would be roses because my mother had a rose bush growing in the back garden. The sight and smell of the roses each summer was beautiful.

key point

Commas are mainly used

- In lists
- In direct speech
- To separate parts of a sentence
- With the word 'however'

- The commas above are used to separate words in a list.

Example 2

'You can't go in there,' Peter shouted.

The comma above is used because it is direct speech. We use the comma to separate what Peter says from the verb describing how he says it.

Example 3

Stacy read the book, but John watched the movie. Even though she didn't want to, Stacy went to the movie later and really enjoyed it. However, she still claims that the book is better.

- The first two commas on the previous page are used to separate two parts of a sentence.
- The last comma is to show that there is a slight pause after the word 'however'.

Time to practise

Rewrite the following paragraph, inserting commas in the correct places.

> Ireland is famous for its green landscape. The country is blessed with thousands of beautiful trees like oak ash hazel and birch. However we have not been looking after the trees or plants. Trees which are good for the environment are cut down for buildings and are not replaced.

Apostrophes

Apostrophes are used:
- To show ownership or possession of something
- To mark the spot of missing letters.

Example 1

> Sarah's smartphone was a lot more expensive than she expected.

- An apostrophe is used here to show that the smartphone belongs to Sarah.

Example 2

> Galway's Eyre Square is the centre of the city and a meeting spot for tourists and locals.

- An apostrophe is used here to show that Eyre Square belongs to or is part of Galway city.

Example 3

> John can't go to the park this evening. He couldn't go to school this morning because he had a cold.

- The apostrophes above are used to replace letters so that the words can be shortened:
  - 'Can't' is short for 'cannot'
  - 'Couldn't' is short for 'could not'.

Time to practise

Insert apostrophes in the correct places in the following piece:

> Abdel looked across the green hills and saw where he must go. He couldnt hike it because it was too dangerous. He would have to fly across the valley if he wanted to get Dalias medical bag to her in time. The last message hed received had said that Alan was bleeding badly, and they needed help. He knew he shouldnt attempt to fly the plane without his father, but he had no choice.

Homophones and commonly confused words

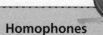

One of the most common issues for writers is confusing words that sound the same.

Some of the following examples are homophones and others are just commonly confused words.

> **Homophones**
> Words that sound the same but can have different meanings and spellings.

- There/they're/their
  - 'There' is used for location – 'The bag is over there.'
  - 'They're' is short for 'They are' – 'They're going to the park tonight.'
  - 'Their' means belonging to them – 'Their bag is in the car.'

Let's put them all together:

They're going into the shopping centre over there to collect their bags.

- Too/two/to
  - 'Too' means 'also' or 'as well' – 'I am going to the park too.'
  - It also means 'more than necessary' – 'I put too much sugar in her tea.'
  - 'Two' is the spelling of the number 2.
  - 'To' has lots of meanings. It can mean to move towards something – 'I ran to the park.'
  - It also can be put with a verb – 'I am going to run to the park.'

Let's put them all together:

Nina and Kyle have gone to the park. The two of us will go to the park too.

- Where/were/we're/wear
  - 'Where' is a question about location – 'Where are you going tonight?'
  - 'Were' is the past plural of the verb 'to be' – 'We were at the cinema last night.'
  - 'We're' is short for 'We are' – 'We're going to the funfair tonight.'
  - 'Wear' is used when talking about clothes – 'What will I wear tonight?'

Let's put them all together:

If we're going where I think we're going, then I'm going to wear wellies because we were jumping in muddy bog holes the last time we were there.

- It's/Its
  - 'It's' is short for 'It is' – 'It's a terrible day.'
  - 'Its' means belonging to something that we have just mentioned or can easily identify – 'I bought a new car. I need to put its number plates on.'

Let's put them both together:

It's a good job you paid for its repair or you would have been in trouble with the Gardaí.

- Your/you're
  - 'Your' means belonging to you – 'Your laces are untied.'
  - 'You're' is short for 'you are' – 'You're going to finish your chores when you get home.'

Let's put them both together:

You're not going to style your hair like that going to the party, are you? Your mother will kill you!

- Could have/would have/should have

The phrases above are not homophones, but they are often used incorrectly because people sometimes write 'could of'/'would of'/'should of'.

The reason for this is simple. When we shorten the phrases (using apostrophes), they become 'could've'/'would've'/'should've'. When we say them out loud, they sound very like 'could of'/'would of'/'should of'. However, to write these phrases like that is incorrect.

I should have told the truth, and I would have if only I could have.

- A lot
  - 'A lot' is often misspelled as one whole word: 'alot'.

There were a lot of people at the concert.

Visit the English Oxford Living Dictionaries online at www.en.oxforddictionaries.com to investigate more commonly confused words and commonly misspelled words.

- Search under Grammar>Usage for a blog post on 'Commonly confused words'.
- Search under Grammar>Spelling for a blog post on 'Common misspellings'.

Time to practise

Write out the following paragraph, correcting any errors you see.

Their where too customers inside the bank when the robbers arrived. They shot there guns into the ceiling and shouted, 'Get down on youre knees'. The customers and staff began screaming and panicking.

'You should of brought the tape,' said one of the robbers. 'Now we can't tie people up or cover theyre mouths.'

'Were's the manager?' the tallest of the robbers shouted. A small, thin man slowly put up his hand and stepped forward nervously.

'Open the safe, now!' shouted the other masked man. The terrified manager went through a small glass door followed closely by the robber.

A few seconds later, the robber shouted, 'Where going too be rich, Steve. Theirs alot of money here.'

'Why are you shouting my name, you idiot?' screamed Steve. 'Let's get out of here.'

Nouns/adjectives/verbs/adverbs

- Nouns – A word that names a person, place, thing or idea.
  - John is a hairdresser.
- Adjective – A word that describes a noun.
  - John is a great hairdresser. (John is not just a hairdresser, he is a *great* hairdresser.)
- Verb – A word that describes an action.
  - Alicia kicked the ball.
- Adverb – A word that describes a verb.
  - Alicia kicked the ball angrily. ('Angrily' shows us *how* Alicia kicked the ball.)

Identify the nouns, adjectives, verbs and adverbs in the following piece. There are:

- 17 nouns
- 8 adjectives
- 16 verbs
- 2 adverbs

> The forest looked a lot darker up-close than Debbie expected. She jumped when she heard the spine-chilling scream again. She stepped slowly past the first tree and felt the squelch of marshy bog below her feet. She took a further step. She felt drops of water falling on her head and shoulders from the shaking trees and worried that her mother would give out to her for getting soaked. The scream came from deep in the forest again and she knew she must go on. She must help her friend.

Solutions for grammar chapter

Capital letters

Correct the following paragraph by including capitals in the correct places:

> David knew he had to get his speech written for the school assembly. His school, Mercy College, was welcoming President Higgins. David was going to say a few words on behalf of his fellow students. His best friend, Sarah, had helped him write most of it, but now he was really nervous and didn't want to make a fool of himself in front of the president.

Capital letters and full stops

Correct the following piece by inserting capital letters and full stops:

> Jeff was the eldest son of Abbie and Tim Wilson. He was top of his class in all his subjects. His English teacher, Mr Taylor, said he could become the new Stephen King. Jeff didn't like the idea of becoming a writer. He wanted to become a professional athlete.

Commas

Rewrite the following paragraph, inserting commas in the correct places:

Ireland is famous for its green landscape. The country is blessed with thousands of beautiful trees like oak, ash, hazel and birch. However, we have not been looking after the trees or plants. Trees, which are good for the environment, are cut down for buildings and are not replaced.

Apostrophes

Insert apostrophes in the correct places in the following piece:

Abdel looked across the green hills and saw where he must go. He couldn't hike it because it was too dangerous. He would have to fly across the valley if he wanted to get Dalia's medical bag to her in time. The last message he'd received had said that Alan was bleeding badly, and they needed help. He knew he shouldn't attempt to fly the plane without his father, but he had no choice.

Final exercise – capital letters, full stops, commas and apostrophes

Write out the following paragraph correcting any errors you see:

There were two customers inside the bank when the robbers arrived. They shot their guns into the ceiling and shouted, 'Get down on your knees.' The customers and staff began screaming and panicking.

'You should have brought the tape,' said one of the robbers. 'Now we can't tie people up or cover their mouths.'

'Where's the manager?' the tallest of the robbers shouted. A small thin man slowly put up his hand and stepped forward nervously.

'Open the safe, now!' shouted the other masked man. The terrified manager went through a small glass door followed closely by the robber.

A few seconds later, the robber shouted, 'We're going to be rich, Steve. There's a lot of money here.'

'Why are you shouting my name, you idiot?' screamed Steve. 'Let's get out of here.'

Nouns/adjectives/verbs/adverbs

The forest looked darker up-close than Debbie expected. She jumped when she heard the spine-chilling scream again. She stepped slowly past the first tree and felt the squelch of marshy bog below her feet. She took a further step. She felt drops of water falling on her head and shoulders from the shaking trees and worried that her mother would give out to her for getting soaked. The scream came from deep in the forest again and she knew she must go on. She must help her friend.

- 17 nouns
- 16 verbs
- 8 adjectives
- 2 adverbs

This chapter includes examples of answers to past exam questions. Each answer has a grade before it and is followed by an examiner's comment. Compare the answers for the different standards and read the examiner's feedback. Applying the examiner's comments to your own answers should help improve your grades and exam technique.

Exam Question 2018 (Junior Cycle 2018, Final Examination, English Ordinary Level)

Section A – Responding to Poetry

Question 1   *20 marks*

SAMPLE ANSWER 1

GRADE: MERIT

Choose a poem you have studied where the poet expresses a strong feeling about something he or she has experienced. You may not use the poem printed on this paper.

(a) Title of poem: *'I Wandered Lonely as a Cloud (The Daffodils)'*

(b) Name of poet: *William Wordsworth*

(c) What was the poet feeling?

The poet in this poem is feeling like he is happy because he is walking by the daffodils and he really likes them because they make him feel good. He likes the way they look and the colour yellow and this makes him happy.

(d) Why do you think the poet was feeling that way?

The poet was feeling that way because he likes the flowers and they make him happy. He sees them beside him as he goes on his walks and they are bright yellow so they probably make him feel happy.

(e) Did you think the poet had chosen a good title for his or her poem? Give a reason for your answer.

Yes, because in the poem there lots and lots of daffodils. The Daffodils title makes sense because the poem is about the flowers and the happyness it has for the poet. I can't think of any better title for it.

(f) Did you like or dislike the poem you have chosen? Explain your answer.

I did like the peom because it was simple and it made me think about summer. The way the poet talks about the daffodils is nice and it makes me think about being outside on a sunny day.

EXAMINER'S COMMENT

The candidate has a good understanding of their studied poem, but the answer would benefit from the use of quotation. The student attempts to use the PIE structure, but it is confused at times. There is a lot of repetition of vocabulary and phrases. There are also a number of spelling and punctuation errors.

SAMPLE ANSWER 2

GRADE: HIGHER MERIT

(a) Title of poem: *'I Wandered Lonely as a Cloud (The Daffodils)'*

(b) Name of poet: *William Wordsworth*

(c) What was the poet feeling?

The poet is feeling relaxed and happy. 'I wandered lonely as a cloud...' The poet feels as light as a cloud as he goes on his walk so this shows he was relaxed. When he sees the daffodils, it makes him really happy because there are so many of them.

(d) Why do you think the poet was feeling that way?

I think the poet was feeling that way because he was so shocked to see so many at the one time. 'Ten thousand saw I at a glance...' This shows that he came across so many in one place and this was really strange and unusual. He never saw so many together in his life and he felt so happy about it.

(e) Did you think the poet had chosen a good title for his or her poem?

I think 'The Daffodils' is a brilliant title for the poem because the poet thinks back on this moment when he is older and sad and lonely. This is a great memory for him and the title makes it all about the flowers. He even imagines seeing them dancing so this is a very happy memory for him.

(f) Did you like or dislike the poem you have chosen?

I really enjoyed the poem because the poet seemed really excited about the daffodils and this made me excited as well. 'Tossing their heads in sprightly dance.' The poet imagines that the daffodils are like people and are dancing.

EXAMINER'S COMMENT

The candidate has responded to all parts of the question very well. The use of quotation is welcome. There is good use of PIE in parts (c), (d) and (e). There is some repetition of vocabulary and the explanation for parts (e) and (f) could be more effective.

Exam Question 2017 (Junior Cycle 2017, Final Examination, English Ordinary Level)

Section C – Choosing the Words and Tone to Use

Question 1   *10 marks*

SAMPLE ANSWER 1

GRADE: ACHIEVED

You have had an unpleasant experience at a big public event that you were really looking forward to, such as a concert or sports event. Write an email in which you describe your experience to either:

A friend

or

The organisers of the event.

Your email should be written in a suitable style.

> Hi Lorcan you won't believe what happened to me the other day. i was at a concert in dublin and i was going with my friends and I tried to get in to the place and they said no. who do they think they are because im 16 and i had proof and everything they made me realy mad and im going to write to them people and tell them what I think of them. We had to go away from the concert and I had no way to get home because my bus was not for ages so I was so angry and i never got to see drake.
>
> Talk to you later,
>
> Bobby

EXAMINER'S COMMENT

The candidate has included suitable content based on the question asked. There is a strong personal tone to the piece. The email address must be included and there is a need for better paragraphing. There are a large number of language errors throughout. Additional content is necessary to bring a more rounded sense to the piece.

SAMPLE ANSWER 2

GRADE: DISTINCTION

You have had an unpleasant experience at a big public event that you were really looking forward to, such as a concert or sports event. Write an email in which you describe your experience to either:

A friend

or

The organisers of the event.

Your email should be written in a suitable style.

> Lorcan123@gmail.com
>
> Re: I'm so angry
>
> Hi Lorcan,
>
> How are ya? I hope you are having a great time over in Orlando. I'm so jealous that you got to go and I'm extra jealous because I had a terrible time at the Drake concert the other day.
>
> I was so excited about going with Cian and Conor because it was the first time we were going to a concert on our own. My dad dropped us all up to Dublin and we went towards the gates to get in. The man at the gate looked at us and said, 'You are not old enough to go in on your own.' I said that we were all 16 and I showed him my age card, but he wouldn't believe me. He wouldn't let us in the gates.
>
> It was too late to call my dad for a lift and we had said we would get the bus home, but the bus wasn't for another four hours. We had to sit outside listening to the music, but we were so angry. I'm thinking of writing an email to someone about it.
>
> Talk to you later,
>
> Bobby

EXAMINER'S COMMENT

This content is carefully chosen and perfectly laid out, with correct use of paragraphs and a strong selection of vocabulary. There are detailed descriptions of events and emotions throughout. There is a good use of direct speech and informal language throughout.

Exam Question 2018 (Junior Cycle 2018, Final Examination, English Ordinary Level)

Section C – Writing for a Variety of Purposes

Question 1   *15 marks*

SAMPLE ANSWER 1

GRADE: ACHIEVED

You and your classmates are going to travel along part of the *Wild Atlantic Way** next weekend. You all meet at break time to try to decide whether to camp or to stay in hotels. You know what you would prefer to do. Write out the talk you would give to persuade your classmates to agree with you.

*The *Wild Atlantic Way* is a route along the west coast of Ireland that is popular with tourists.

> Hi everyone,
>
> Im really excited about going to the wild atlantic way next week. Id really like to go to the cliffs of moher because everyone knows it and I haven't been there and I think we should all go because its fun and very high. We can walk along the cliffs and look at the sea and it will be pretty. We can stay in a hotel and have fun at night because we will be talking and playing games. This is why I think we should go.

EXAMINER'S COMMENT

The content and style are suitable for a talk; however, the focus of the talk is the cliffs rather than the accommodation. There is an attempt to use language that gets a reaction with words like 'excited' and 'fun'. There is a need for more language that appeals to people's emotions and a much more organised approach using PIE. There are a number of language errors and poorly expressed points.

SAMPLE ANSWER 2

GRADE: DISTINCTION

You and your classmates are going to travel along part of the *Wild Atlantic Way** next weekend. You all meet at break time to try to decide whether to camp or to stay in hotels. You know what you would prefer to do. Write out the talk you would give to persuade your classmates to agree with you.

*The *Wild Atlantic Way* is a route along the west coast of Ireland that is popular with tourists.

Hi everyone,

I hope you are as excited as I am about our trip next week. I know there are lots of different places to go and I'm really looking forward to the Cliffs of Moher. We must decide on where we are staying and I believe we should camp along the way.

Camping is just more fun than staying in a hotel. We can go from tent to tent without worrying about disturbing our neighbours. We can have our breakfast whenever we want and we can take a walk in the cool night breeze. It will be so crazy.

We are only students and we need to save money. The campsites only cost €20 a tent, but the hotel could cost over €60. Wouldn't it be better to save our money so we can spend it on things we will enjoy? We could buy souvenirs for our families. Not!

It makes sense to do this. If we want to see all of the Wild Atlantic Way, then we need to save our money. We can do it all while looking at the stars.

EXAMINER'S COMMENT

This answer is really well-focused on the question asked. There are two well-explained points in support of the speaker's argument. There is great use of language that gets an emotional reaction and the use of a rhetorical question is excellent. There is a strong personal voice and a good level of informal language.

Exam Question 2018 (Junior Cycle 2018, Final Examination, English Ordinary Level)

Section B – Reading and Responding Imaginatively

Question 1   *25 marks*

SAMPLE ANSWER 1

GRADE: ACHIEVED

Read parts (c), (d), (e) and (f) below and then choose a novel or short story you have studied.

(a) Name of novel or short story: *The Dare*

(b) Author: *?*

(c) If you could ask a character from your chosen text an interesting question about something he or she did, what would the question be?

Name of character: *Danny*

What is the interesting question you would ask?

Why did you hide under Andys bed in the hospital?

(d) What answer do you think the character would give? You may answer as the character.

I think danny hided under andys bed because he didnt went to meet his parents and he was scared.

(e) Would you like to have this character as a friend? Give a reason for your answer.

No I dont think i'd like to have danny as a friend. He ran off on his family wen they really needed him.

EXAMINER'S COMMENT

The candidate answers each question asked and shows a reasonable knowledge of the text. Author name is left blank. The question is not as imaginative as it could be. There are multiple punctuation and expression errors. Part (d) needs further illustration as to why the character was scared. Part (e) lacks evidence to show the character's family needed him.

SAMPLE ANSWER 2

GRADE: DISTINCTION

Read parts (c), (d), (e) and (f) below and then choose a novel or short story you have studied.

(a) Name of novel or short story: *The Dare*

(b) Author: *John Boyne*

(c) If you could ask a character from your chosen text an interesting question about something he or she did, what would the question be?

Name of character: *Danny*

What is the interesting question you would ask?

What was the scariest thing about running away from home?

(d) What answer do you think the character would give? You may answer as the character.

Danny: The scariest thing about running away was being on my own in some really frightening places. Hiding behind the sports hall wasn't too bad, but the night I slept in the car park was really frightening. I always thought some crazy person would find me and kidnap me. I was scared, cold and hungry but I knew I needed to get away because no one cared about me at home. I was so happy that Pete found me in the park.

(e) Would you like to have this character as a friend? Give a reason for your answer.

Yes, I would like to have Danny as a friend because Danny stands up for things he feels strongly about. He stood up for his mum in the hospital when

Andys mum was giving out about her. This showed he loved his mother. He ran away when his dad slapped him. This showed he would not take that from his dad, even though his dad apologised.

EXAMINER'S COMMENT

The answer is largely without error. An apostrophe is left out in part (e) and the second sentence in the same part is poorly phrased. Answers are well explained using the PIE structure. There is a clear knowledge of the text. Good range of vocabulary on show.

Exam Question 2017 (Junior Cycle 2017, Final Examination, English Ordinary Level)

Section A – Reading and Responding Imaginatively

Question 1   *20 marks*

SAMPLE ANSWER 1

GRADE: ACHIEVED

You have been given the job of directing a film or play that you have studied.

(a) Name the film or play that you have studied: *Film: School of Rock*

(b) Name an important character from your chosen film or play: *Zack*

(c) Describe a key moment in the film or play where your named character plays a significant role.

   The key moment I have choosen is the concert at the end. Zack plays a solo on the guitar and the kids win playing their song.

(d) Did you like or dislike what your named character did in the key moment you have described? Give a reason for your answer.

   I really liked what zack did in this scene he plays a solo on the guitar and he looks cool in his outfit. The crowd loved him and were screaming his name.

(e) Give one piece of advice to an actor playing the part of your named character, about how he or she should act during this key moment. Why do you think this piece of advice would help the actor to play the part well?

   I think the actor would be excited so i would tell him to act excited.

EXAMINER'S COMMENT

The candidate has responded accurately to nearly all questions. There is an absence of detail in parts (c) and (d). The candidate has not responded correctly to part (e). They have focused on the actor's emotions generally rather than suggesting actions which help the actor play the part. There are a number of spelling and punctuation errors.

SAMPLE ANSWER 2

GRADE: HIGHER MERIT
You have been given the job of directing a film or play that you have studied.

(a) Name the film or play that you have studied: *Film: School of Rock*

(b) Name an important character from your chosen film or play: *Dewey*

(c) Describe a key moment in the film or play where your named character plays a significant role.

The key moment I have chosen is when Dewey gets caught out by the police and Ms mullins for not being a real teacher. All the teachers are supposed to be at the open night. Dewey is trying to explain to the parents about all the things they have learnt in class, but he can't explain anything about class cause they only play music. The kids tell him to tell their parents about the competition. Then the police arrive with his flatmates and they tell Ms mullins and the parents that he's not a real teacher. He says some really weird stuff and ends up running away.

(d) Did you like or dislike what your named character did in the key moment you have described? Give a reason for your answer.

I liked what dewey did because he was really funny. He just starts listing subjects to the parents and tells them, 'it's been covered'. He hasn't a clue what he's talking about. He begins to sweat cause he sees the police and starts going on about the competition. I also liked how he complimented the kids. He says Zack is an 'insane guitar player' and 'Gordon is a genius'. This showed that he was now a kinder person.

(e) Give one piece of advice to an actor playing the part of your named character, about how he or she should act during this key moment. Why do you think this piece of advice would help the actor to play the part well?

I think I would tell the actor to fidget a lot. Dewey is very nervous during this moment and I think he fidgets a lot.

EXAMINER'S COMMENT

The candidate shows a very good knowledge of the text and has described the key moment in a lot of detail. All parts of the question are attempted, and answers are well supported with evidence from the text. There are a number of spelling and punctuation errors. While correction of the spelling and punctuation errors would improve the overall grade, a distinction could be achieved with a greater variety of vocabulary and less informality in parts (c) and (d). There is also room for more effective **description** of events and further quotation.

Reflection note: Self-assessment sheet

Self-assessment sheet

School	Student
	Today's Date
Title of Work	Genre

I worked on my own ☐

I worked in a group ☐ with (names) _____

Reflect on your work and then answer the questions below

(*For an individual piece of work*) What I learned while doing this work:

(*For group work*) What I learned from my classmates while doing this work:

Two things I did well:

One thing that could be improved on:

What I would do differently next time (link this to the area that you would like to improve):

Appendix: Learning Outcomes

The Learning Outcomes are very important as these determine what will be assessed at the different assessment moments. The following pages highlight which Learning Outcomes are assessed at particular assessment moments.

Assessment moment 1

Classroom-Based Assessment 1: Oral Communication

Eight Learning Outcomes are assessed in particular through **Oral Communication**. They are:

Oral Learning Outcomes
1. Know and use the conventions of oral language interaction, in a variety of contexts, including class groups, for a range of purposes, such as asking for information, stating an opinion, listening to others, informing, explaining, arguing, persuading, criticising, commentating, narrating, imagining and speculating
5. Deliver a short oral text, alone and/or in collaboration with others, using appropriate language, style and visual content for specific audiences and chosen purposes
7. Choose appropriate language, style and visual content for specific audiences and chosen purposes: persuading, informing, narrating, describing a process
9. Apply what they have learned about the effectiveness of spoken texts to their own use of oral language
13. Develop their spoken language proficiency by experimenting with word choice, being creative with syntax, being precise, and stimulating appropriate responses relative to context and purpose
Reading Learning Outcomes
3. Use a wide range of reading comprehension strategies appropriate to texts, including digital texts: to retrieve information; to link to previous knowledge, follow a process or argument, summarise, link main ideas; to monitor their own understanding; to question, analyse, synthesise and evaluate
Writing Learning Outcomes
3. Write for a variety of purposes, for example to analyse, evaluate, imagine, explore, engage, amuse, narrate, inform, explain, argue, persuade, criticise, comment on what they have heard, viewed and read
5. Engage with and learn from models of oral and written language use to enrich their own written work

Assessment moment 2

Classroom-Based Assessment 2: My Collection of Texts

11 Learning Outcomes are assessed in particular through the **Collection of Texts**. They are:

Oral Learning Outcomes

1. Know and use the conventions of oral language interaction, in a variety of contexts, including class groups, for a range of purposes, such as asking for information, stating an opinion, listening to others, informing, explaining, arguing, persuading, criticising, commentating, narrating, imagining and speculating

Reading Learning Outcomes

2. Read for a variety of purposes: learning, pleasure, research and comparison

6. Read their texts for understanding and appreciation of character, setting, story and action: to explore how and why characters develop, and to recognise the importance of setting and plot structure

8. Read their texts to understand and appreciate language enrichment by examining an author's choice of words, the use and effect of simple figurative language, vocabulary and language patterns, and images, as appropriate to the text

Writing Learning Outcomes

1. Demonstrate their understanding that there is a clear purpose for all writing activities and be able to plan, draft, redraft, and edit their own writing as appropriate

2. Discuss their own and other students' written work constructively and with clear purpose

3. Write for a variety of purposes, for example to analyse, evaluate, imagine, explore, engage, amuse, narrate, inform, explain, argue, persuade, criticise, and comment on what they have heard, viewed and read

4. Write competently in a range of text forms, for example letter, report, multi-modal text, review, blog, using appropriate vocabulary, tone and a variety of styles to achieve a chosen purpose for different audiences

6. Use editing skills continuously during the writing process to enhance meaning and impact: select vocabulary, reorder words, phrases and clauses, correct punctuation and spelling, reorder paragraphs, remodel, manage content

9. Engage in the writing process as a private, pleasurable and purposeful activity and using a personal voice as their individual style is thoughtfully developed over the years

11. Use language conventions appropriately, especially punctuation and spelling, to aid meaning and presentation and to enhance the reader's experience

Assessment moment 4

The final exam

A selection of **23 Learning Outcomes** are assessed on the **final 2-hour exam**.

In the table below, the red numbers indicate the oral, reading and writing Learning Outcomes for the final exam.

ORAL

1	2	3	4	5	6	7	8	9	10	11	12	13

READING

1	2	3	4	5	6	7	8	9	10	11	12	13

WRITING

1	2	3	4	5	6	7	8	9	10	11	12	13

23 Learning Outcomes for the final exam

Oral Learning Outcomes

8. Listen actively in order to interpret meaning, compare, evaluate effectiveness of, and respond to drama, poetry, media broadcasts, digital media, noting key ideas, style, tone, content and overall impact in a systematic way

12. Demonstrate how register, including grammar, text structure and word choice, varies with context and purpose in spoken texts

Reading Learning Outcomes

1. Read texts with fluency, understanding and competence, decoding groups of words/phrases and not just single words

2. Read for a variety of purposes: learning, pleasure, research, comparison

3. Use a wide range of reading comprehension strategies appropriate to texts, including digital texts: to retrieve information; to link to previous knowledge, follow a process or argument, summarise, link main ideas; to monitor their own understanding; to question, analyse, synthesise and evaluate

4. Use an appropriate critical vocabulary while responding to literary texts

13. Appreciate a variety of registers and understand their use in the written context

12. Understand how word choice, syntax, grammar and text structure may vary with context and purpose

11. Identify and comment on features of English at word and sentence level using appropriate terminology, showing how such features contribute to overall effect

9. Identify, appreciate and compare the ways in which different literary, digital and visual genres and sub-genres shape texts and shape the reader's experience of them

8. Read their texts to understand and appreciate language enrichment by examining an author's choice of words, the use and effect of simple figurative language, vocabulary and language patterns and images, as appropriate to the text

6. Read their texts for understanding and appreciation of character, setting, story and action: to explore how and why characters develop, and to recognise the importance of setting and plot structure

7. Select key moments from their texts and give thoughtful value judgements on the main character, a key scene, a favourite image from a film, a poem, a drama, a chapter, a media or web-based event

1. Demonstrate their understanding that there is a clear purpose for all writing activities and be able to plan, draft, redraft and edit their own writing as appropriate

3. Write for a variety of purposes, for example to analyse, evaluate, imagine, explore, engage, amuse, narrate, inform, explain, argue, persuade, criticise, comment on what they have heard, viewed and read

4. Write competently in a range of text forms, for example letter, report, multi-modal text, review, blog, using appropriate vocabulary, tone and a variety of styles to achieve a chosen purpose for different audiences

12. Demonstrate an understanding of how syntax, grammar, text structure and word choice may vary with context and purpose

6. Use editing skills continuously during the writing process to enhance meaning and impact: select vocabulary, reorder words, phrases and clauses, correct punctuation and spelling, reorder paragraphs, remodel, manage content

Writing Learning Outcomes

11. Use language conventions appropriately, especially punctuation and spelling, to aid meaning and presentation and to enhance the reader's experience

7. Respond imaginatively in writing to their texts, showing a critical appreciation of language, style and content, choice of words, language patterns, tone, images

10. Use and apply their knowledge of language structures, for example, sentence structure, paragraphing, grammar, to make their writing a richer experience for themselves and the reader

9. Engage in the writing process as a private, pleasurable and purposeful activity and using a personal voice as their individual style is thoughtfully developed over the years

8. Write about the effectiveness of key moments from their texts, commenting on characters, key scenes, favourite images from a film, a poem, a drama, a chapter, a media or web-based event

Acknowledgements

The authors and publisher are grateful to the following for permission to reproduce copyrighted material:

'Mid-Term Break' from *Death of a Naturalist* by Seamus Heaney. Copyright © Seamus Heaney, 1966, 1991, Faber and Faber Ltd.

'I Believe in Unicorns' from *Singing for Mrs Pettigrew* by Michael Morpurgo. Copyright © Michael Morpurgo (2007). Reproduced by permission of David Higham Associates.

Extract from *A Monster Calls* by Patrick Ness based on an original idea by Siobhan Dowd and illustrated by Jim Kay. Reproduced by permission of Walker Books Ltd, London SE11 5HJ. www.walker.co.uk

'Winter days' from *The Fox on the Roundabout* by Gareth Owen. Published by Macmillan Children's, 2001. Copyright © Gareth Owen. Reproduced by permission of the author c/o Rogers, Coleridge & White Ltd., 20 Powis Mews, London W11 1JN.

'The New Kid on the Block' by Jack Prelutsky. Text Copyright © 1984 by Jack Prelutsky. Used by permission of HarperCollins Publishers.

Extract from Writing Genre – A Structured Approach by PDST. Copyright © PDST, 2013.

The authors and publisher have made every effort to trace all copyright holders, but if any have been inadvertently overlooked we would be pleased to make the necessary arrangement at the first opportunity.